It is in the daily pursuit of God where we feel most alive, for it is there that we encounter why we were created. *Wondrous Pursuit* will stir a hunger within you to know God more and draw you closer to Jesus as you walk daily with Him. I'm grateful that Jarrid Wilson has taken the time to invite us into a deeper journey with God.

BANNING LIEBSCHER
founder and pastor of Jesus Culture

Hopefully all of us have people in our lives whom we experience as a breath of fresh air. For me, Jarrid Wilson is such a person. Jarrid is a young leader who is wise, generous, humble and kind beyond his years. Beneath his handsome exterior lies a childlike, old soul, in the best sense of the word. He is keenly in touch with the human condition. He knows, and cares deeply, that people are lonely, disconnected and much afraid, and is not afraid to move into those spaces with presence and encouragement. And yet Jarrid is no cynic. More than just about anyone else I know, he is a young man filled with wonder: wonder at the image of God in every person, and wonder at the grandeur and grace of God Himself. In this approachable little book, Jarrid invites us to share in that experience of wonder. Pick it up. Commit to reading it over a period of time. I think you'll be glad that you did.

SCOTT SAULS
senior minister, Christ Presbyterian Church (Nashville);
author of *Jesus Outside the Lines* and *Befriend*

Faith should be a buoyant force that lifts us into the stratosphere, but it is often a millstone that sinks us to the depths. Jarrid Wilson reminds us that faith is easier than we assume, that grace is freer than we believe, and that God is more majestic than we know. If you're worn out from striving for God's affection, then *Wondrous Pursuit* is for you. It will liberate you with this stunning truth: When you decide to chase after the Almighty, you will discover that you are already home.

JONATHAN MERRITT

antic;
gined

Jarrid's pursuit of God is contagious! His passion for Jesus and people is so evident in all he does. He's the real deal. Not sure how to pursue God yourself? Going through a dry season in your relationship with Jesus? Want to set your heart on fire even more for God? Spend the next 30 days with Jarrid pursuing our wondrous God.

ADAM WEBER
lead pastor, Embrace Church (Sioux Falls, SD);
author of *Talking With God*

A. W. Tozer said, "To have found God and still pursue Him is the soul's paradox of love." In every generation, there are people who feel this tug on their heart, people with an inner longing, who spend their days on a soul's pursuit of the only One who can satisfy. Jarrid Wilson writes for a new generation who sense this inner longing for The Wondrous Pursuit, and cry out with the psalmist, "My soul thirsts for God, for the living God. When can I go and meet with God?" (Psalm 42:2)

MATT BROWN
evangelist; founder, Think Eternity;
author of *Revolutionaries* and *Awakening*

Our souls were made to pursue and be pursued by God. This isn't a one-time thing or something we move on from. It is a daily discipline of spending time with Jesus. They say it takes 30 days to build a habit, and Jarrid is giving you an incredible tool to help you build a habit of pursuing God in response to his pursuit of you.

STEPHEN MILLER
author of *Liberating King* and
Worship Leaders, We Are Not Rock Stars

Jarrid invites us into a journey of not just more information about God but a wondrous pursuit of the heart of God that brings transformation. *Wondrous Pursuit* is a devotional that will allow you to discover God's love and be changed by it.

JUSTIN DAVIS
coauthor of *Beyond Ordinary*;
founder of RefineUs Ministries;
pastor at Hope City Church (Indianapolis)

Jarrid is a thoughtful young man who is asking important questions and offering insightful answers.

JAMIE GEORGE
pastor, Journey Church;
author of *Love Well* and *Poets & Saints*

In *Wondrous Pursuit*, Jarrid Wilson takes the reader on a journey of the heart, mind, and soul. His words are timely and his approach is accessible. The devotions are a daily feast for the spiritually hungry. Anyone who desires to shape their lives by the natural rhythms of God's love and grace will find Jarrid a helpful guide and his writings a road map to a deeper life in Jesus.

IAN DIORIO
lead pastor, Yucaipa Christian Church;
author of *Trivial Pursuits*

There is no more wondrous pursuit than the life that God has for you. Jarrid Wilson knows that and has been on that pursuit. This devotional will be an encouragement and guide from an experienced traveler. I could not be more excited for all who will go on this journey.

CHUCK BOOHER
senior pastor, Crossroads Christian Church (Corona, CA)

It seems to me that there are two great characteristics of those who remain steadfast in faith and love: rest in the Gospel, and desperation for Jesus. These twin factors keep us rooted in grace and longing for the beauty to which such a gift summons us. My friend Jarrid Wilson has penned a devotional that will reinforce both of these qualities, his words pointing us to the Scriptures and then, through their testimony, to the One who is our life. Let's face it: We get weary at times, and our hearts can grow cold. When that occurs, our souls need a merciful wakeup call, followed by a sustained course in gospel grace and Jesus-focused discipleship. That's what *Wondrous Pursuit* provides. Don't just enjoy it; hear it! And let these pages ignite your heart for a fresh pursuit of the Holy.

DAVID PATRICK CASSIDY
lead pastor, Christ Community Church (Franklin, TN)

We all need some "wonder" in our daily experience with God. We are all looking for a fresh newness in our pursuit of God, and this is where Jarrid has given us a great gift. After spending time in the pages of *Wondrous Pursuit,* I leave with a sense of freshness, awe, and knowing, in the deepest parts of my soul, how wondrous the pursuit of God truly is. This is such a fresh word to those in dry places and to bring hope to the work of Jesus in our lives daily. Thank you, Jarrid!

JOSH HAWK
pastor, The Move Church (Nashville, TN)

Pursuing God is crucial for everyone—whether someone exploring the Christian faith or someone who has been studying things of God for years. In Jarrid Wilson's wonderful new devotional, you'll find thought-provoking passages of Scripture paired with insightful commentary. This devotional will take you further on the journey of pursuit!

SHAUNTI FELDHAHN
social researcher; author, *For Women Only*

I have read and been spiritually challenged by all of Jarrid's books. Reading his books has always demanded a personal response. They've forced me to take my spiritual walk with Jesus seriously. *Wondrous Pursuit* was certainly no different. The daily devotions are a reminder of who Jesus is and who we can be through him. Anyone who is looking to be shaped daily by God's promises should read this book.

JEFF HUXFORD, MD
blogger at Finding Normal (JeffHuxford.com)

Jarrid Wilson is a creative, Jesus-loving, pioneer of the Christian faith. This devotional will not just encourage some but inspire many to live out their God-sized dreams and callings in life. I encourage others to utilize this study to dive deep into God's Word and truly pursue His best in their lives!

JOSH HUSMANN
lead pastor, Mercy Road Church (Carmel, IN)

DAILY ENCOUNTERS WITH
AN ALMIGHTY GOD

Also by Jarrid Wilson:

30 Words: A Devotional for the Rest of Us

Learn more at KirkdalePress.com/authors/jarrid-wilson

wondrous pursuit

DAILY ENCOUNTERS WITH
AN ALMIGHTY GOD

A 30-DAY DEVOTIONAL

JARRID WILSON

KIRKDALE PRESS

Print ISBN 9781683590088
Digital ISBN 9781683590095

Kirkdale Editorial: Justin Marr, Rebecca Florence Miller,
     Lynnea Smoyer, Abigail Stocker
Cover Design: Jarrid Wilson
Back Cover Design: Liz Donovan
Typesetting: ProjectLuz.com

To my boys

May you always remember God's wondrous love for you

CONTENTS

INTRODUCTION

The pursuit of God is a pursuit full of excitement, transformation, adventure, and inner discovery. In it, we cling to the truths we know, yet hold on to faith for the answers still unveiled. The magnificence that is God acts as our light in a world that has become so dark. God, our creator and life-breathing orchestrator, provides the wisdom and knowledge necessary to truly find a life of fulfillment and promise. Let your pursuit of God be a wondrous pursuit, a story worth telling, and a daring experience worth reliving day after day.

The pursuit of God has many facets—including prayer, worship, church, community, meditation, servanthood, and grace. Throughout this book you will have the opportunity to reflect on various passages within the Bible that pertain to your walk with God and each of these facets. You'll have the opportunity to truly evaluate the strength of your spiritual roots and to find out more about the foundation you've chosen to build your life upon. Whether you have been studying God's word for the last fifty years, as little as a few days, or have yet to open up a Bible at all, I pray the words in this book will enrich your life.

No one's pursuit of God is perfect. In fact, we're all going to have a pursuit that's messy and unique and in need of God's grace and direction. But that's the beauty of God; he yearns for our pursuit even though it is full of impurities and imperfection. Our purpose in pursuing God is simple: because he has chosen to first pursue us. No matter who we are, what we've done, or where we've once been, our creator and Father in heaven is constantly and radically pursuing us on a day-to-day basis. Why? Because just like any other well-intentioned relationship, you pursue those you love and care about. In this pursuit you get to know more about that person each and every day you spend time with them.

God, being the creator of the universe, has nothing more he needs to know about us, but he still chooses to pursue us anyway. For the next 30 days, I would encourage you to drop any preconceived ideas you may have about this devotional, open your heart for an opportunity to grow, and let down your guard so that God can begin molding and shaping your heart.

I cannot begin to explain the wondrous journey I found myself embarking on while writing this devotional, and I pray God will speak to you in the same way he has to me—in exponential love, grace, and wisdom. The next month is going to be just one of the many opportunities you will have in life to deepen and widen your spiritual roots, but I pray you fully take the opportunity at hand to be diligent in reading for the next 30 days.

So whether you will be journeying through this pursuit by yourself or with friends, loved ones, or even a small group of fellow believers, I pray that you will open your heart to the endless possibilities of God's love and truth. There is never an end point when it comes to pursuing God. There is no final lap or finish line to cross. The wondrous pursuit of God is one of unending treasure and discovery; it continuously transforms us from the inside out in a way that no one but God ever could.

DAY 1.
WAKE UP, SLEEPER

Ephesians 5:1–14

Therefore become imitators of God, as beloved children, and live in love, just as also Christ loved us, and gave himself for us an offering and sacrifice to God for a fragrant smell. But sexual immorality, and all uncleanness, or greediness, must not even be named among you (as is fitting for saints), and obscenity, and foolish talk, or coarse jesting (which are not proper), but rather thanksgiving. For this you know for certain, that every sexually immoral person, or unclean person, or greedy person (who is an idolater), does not have an inheritance in the kingdom of Christ and God. Let no one deceive you with empty words, for because of these things the wrath of God is coming on the sons of disobedience.

Therefore do not be sharers with them, for you were formerly darkness, but now you are light in the Lord. Live like children of light (for the fruit of the light is in all goodness and righteousness and truth), trying to learn what is well-pleasing to the Lord. And do not participate in the unfruitful deeds of darkness, but rather even expose them. For it is shameful even to speak about the things being done by them in secret, but all things exposed by the light are made visible, for everything made visible is light. Therefore it says,

Wake up, sleeper,
and rise from the dead,
and Christ will shine on you.

Therefore, consider carefully how you live, not as unwise but as wise, making the most of the time because the days are evil.

Have you ever stopped to think about what it means when someone says they're *pursuing* God? "Pursuit" is a powerful word. It's so much more than simply "following" God. People who are pursuing God aren't lagging behind, showing up late, or halfheartedly chasing after him. They're all in.

Fervently, passionately, unwaveringly *in*.

The Merriam-Webster dictionary actually says that to "pursue" means "to follow and try to catch or capture (someone or something) for usually a long distance or time."[1] When we truly pursue God, we're out to catch his incomprehensible attributes of love, grace, and mercy. We're to put away selfish desires and instead put on the likeness and wonder of God.

So how do we do it? What does this wondrous pursuit actually look like? Where do we start? What do we do—or not do? In Ephesians 5:1–4, Paul writes clear instructions for people who are pursuing God: Imitate God in all that you do; follow his example; offer yourself fully to him as he offered his Son, Jesus, fully to us.

WE'RE TOLD TO WAKE UP, RISE WITH CHRIST FROM DEATH TO LIFE.

We're told to wake up, rise with Christ from death to life, and see his light shine upon us. It's the beginning of a wondrous pursuit that lasts a lifetime.

Pursuing God means doing away with selfish desires and detours that might get in the way. It means fully embracing the beauty of God and allowing his love to change us entirely.

Going "all in" would be another way to put it—jumping headfirst into a life that seeks to not only glorify God, but please him. Putting the desires of God before your own and before others. Making God the center of your life—a center around which you choose to revolve, the point on which you build everything else.

GO FURTHER

What does it mean to "live in the light"?

_____

_____

_____

_____

Does your life currently exude the light you're living in? If so, explain why. If not, explain what you can change in order to make this a reality.

_____

_____

_____

_____

How can we imitate God on a daily basis? Will we ever be able to fully embody each and every one of his unique characteristics?

_____

_____

_____

_____

_____

DAY 2.
CHASING SIGNPOSTS

1 Corinthians 1:18–31

For the message about the cross is foolishness to those who are perishing, but to us who are being saved it is the power of God. For it is written,

> *"I will destroy the wisdom of the wise,*
> *and the intelligence of the intelligent I will confound."*

Where is the wise person? Where is the scribe? Where is the debater of this age? Has not God made foolish the wisdom of the world? For since, in the wisdom of God, the world through its wisdom did not know God, God was pleased through the foolishness of preaching to save those who believe. For indeed, Jews ask for sign miracles and Greeks seek wisdom, but we preach Christ crucified, to the Jews a cause for stumbling, but to the Gentiles foolishness, but to those who are called, both Jews and Greeks, Christ is the power of God and the wisdom of God. For the foolishness of God is wiser than human wisdom, and the weakness of God is stronger than human strength.

For consider your calling, brothers, that not many were wise according to human standards, not many were powerful, not many were well born. But the foolish things of the world God chose in order that he might put to shame the wise, and the weak things of the world God chose in order that he might put to shame the strong, and the insignificant of the world, and the despised, God chose, the things that are not, in order that he might abolish the things that are, so that all flesh may not boast before God. But from him you are in Christ Jesus, who became wisdom to us from God, and righteousness and sanctification and redemption, so that, just as it is written, "The one who boasts, let him boast in the Lord."

I love studying different viewpoints on the Bible. I love finding ways to deepen my relationship with God. And I love looking for new perspectives that make me think more broadly. It's a true joy to follow the writings and teachings of fellow pastors and leaders, and the content available today is vast. If you take the time, you can learn so much from Christian thinkers like C. S. Lewis, Dietrich Bonhoeffer, and Eugene Peterson. But although these men's writings show incredible wisdom in their biblical understanding, even they would likely tell you, "For the foolishness of God is wiser than human wisdom" (1 Cor 1:25 NIV).

No matter how deep and insightful Christianity's best minds may be, they pale in comparison to God's wisdom. While theology and academics can help enrich our understanding of God and his word, scholarly wisdom should not be the sole object of our pursuit. These are only signposts on our chase for the main goal: Jesus. Building our spiritual houses on top of human-made foundations will surely lead us to eventual destruction, but building upon the beauty and omnipotence of God will surely keep us standing tall generation after generation.

We're reminded in 1 Corinthians 1:18–30 that God didn't hone his message for the wise, influential elite. Instead, he "chose the foolish things of the world" (v. 27 NIV)—the weak things, the lowly and despised. He did this, Paul writes, "so that no one may boast before him" (v. 29 NIV). We can't claim to "get" God's love on any account of our own. It's not something that we just happen to be smart enough to understand or forward-thinking enough to implement. It all comes from God. All we can do is chase after him, looking to the cross for whatever ounce of knowledge or experience of God we might gain.

NO MATTER HOW DEEP AND INSIGHTFUL CHRISTIANITY'S BEST MINDS MAY BE, THEY PALE IN COMPARISON TO GOD'S WISDOM.

Theology, worship music, devotionals, small groups—these can be wonderful tools for enhancing our relationship with God. But on their own, they'll never be enough to provide a true and enriching relationship with God. On their own, they will always fail to live up to the true depth that is the gospel. Examine your heart and ask whether you're pursuing *God* or pursuing the things that serve as *signposts* on the way to him.

GO FURTHER

Do you have a favorite author or biblical teacher? What about this person do you enjoy? What characteristics does she or he have that you seek for your own life?

_____

_____

_____

_____

_____

What things do you find yourself chasing rather than God?

_____

_____

_____

_____

Other than the things noted above, what types of signposts do you find yourself tempted to chase on a daily basis?

_____

_____

_____

_____

_____

How can we make sure that our spiritual foundations are truly in Christ?

_____

_____

_____

_____

_____

DAY 3.
WHO ARE YOU FOLLOWING?

Galatians 1:6–24

I am astonished that you are turning away so quickly from the one who called you by the grace of Christ to a different gospel, not that there is a different gospel, except there are some who are disturbing you and wanting to distort the gospel of Christ. But even if we or an angel from heaven should proclaim a gospel to you contrary to what we proclaimed to you, let him be accursed! As we said before, and now I say again, if anyone is proclaiming a gospel to you contrary to what you have received, let him be accursed! For am I now making an appeal to people or to God? Or am I seeking to please people? If I were still trying to please people, I would not be a slave of Christ.

For I make known to you, brothers, the gospel that has been proclaimed by me, that it is not of human origin. For neither did I receive it from man, nor was I taught it, but I received it through a revelation of Jesus Christ. For you have heard about my former way of life in Judaism, that to an extraordinary degree I was persecuting the church of God, and trying to destroy it, and was progressing in Judaism beyond many contemporaries in my nation, because I was a far more zealous adherent of the traditions handed down by my forefathers.

But when the one who set me apart from my mother's womb and called me by his grace was pleased to reveal his Son in me in order that I would proclaim the gospel about him among the Gentiles, immediately I did not consult with flesh and blood, nor did I go up to Jerusalem to those who were apostles before me, but I went away to Arabia and I returned again to Damascus. Then after three years I went up to Jerusalem to become acquainted with Cephas, and I stayed with him fifteen days, but I did not see any others of the apostles except James, the brother of the Lord. (Now the things which I am writing to you, behold, I assure you before God that I am not lying.) Then I came to the regions of Syria and of Cilicia, but I was unknown in person to the churches of Judea that are in Christ, and they were only hearing, "The one formerly persecuting us is now proclaiming the faith that formerly he was attempting to destroy," and they were glorifying God because of me.

Before his eyes were opened to the truth, the apostle Paul (then known as Saul) was well known for violently killing and persecuting Christians (see Gal 1:23). Once he had his dramatic encounter with God, however, he fervently switched gears and began the wondrous pursuit of Jesus. His story is one of beauty and radical grace. The two lives he lived are drastically different in comparison, but that's the transformative power of God—he can do that.

In today's reading, Paul tells the church in Galatia that as soon as the truth of Jesus was revealed to him, "immediately I did not consult with flesh and blood [any human being, NIV]." Instead of going to Jerusalem, where he could learn from other apostles, Paul immediately went away to Arabia. He didn't think twice about his next step. He encountered God and then immediately shared about his transformation.

So intense was Paul's pursuit of God that he was willing to follow God's lead wherever it took him. That's something each of us should dwell on if we claim to follow Jesus. Paul didn't do what was comfortable, natural, or easy. He traveled the world telling others about Jesus.

Paul was all in on the wondrous pursuit. Are you? Am I? Are we really in this 100 percent? Do we ever hesitate or withdraw?

There's so much to see in the little window into Paul's life that this passage gives us. I encourage you to spend some time with this passage and open yourself up to what God has to show you in his word.

Verse 10 offers another element of Paul's wondrous pursuit that stands out to me. "If I were still trying to please people," he writes, "I would not be a servant of Christ" (NIV). Pleasing people isn't found in any drop of what it means to be immersed in the Christian life. It's simply contrary to the calling we've been given.

OUR WORTH IS TO BE FOUND IN GOD, SOUGHT IN GOD, AND ROOTED IN GOD.

Paul wasn't worried about living for the approval of others. Why? Because living for others' approval is a draining process that will never harvest eternal fulfillment. I'll be the first to admit that I'm a people pleaser, and I've always had a hard time hearing that someone doesn't like me. But the reality is, even Jesus has people who don't like him. Not everyone is going to see eye to eye with my way of living, my writing, my beliefs, or my pursuit. And I'm okay with that.

Today, I encourage you to take a step back and look at the bigger picture of life. We're all children of God, and that is where we should find our worth. If we fail to do so, we will never find true value or identity. Instead, we'll be running around life like a chicken without a head—lost, aimless, and confused. Our worth is to be found in God, sought in God, and rooted in God.

This said, what or whom are you pursuing? Are you, like Paul, trying to please Jesus, or are you searching for someone else's approval? This is something we must reflect on each and every day of our pursuit. Our daily response should be to deny our selfish desires and instead pursue what's next in our journey with God.

GO FURTHER

To what/whom in your life do you currently give most of your time? Does this thing/person help or hinder your relationship with God?

_____

_____

_____

_____

_____

Think of a time you elevated something higher than God. Did it work out? What did you learn from that experience?

_____

_____

_____

_____

_____

Write down two or three things that you once pursued or still are pursuing more than your relationship with God.

_____

_____

_____

_____

_____

DAY 4.
CITIZENS OF HEAVEN

Philippians 1:18–27

But also I will rejoice, for I know that this will turn out to me for deliverance through your prayer and the support of the Spirit of Jesus Christ, according to my eager expectation and hope, that I will be put to shame in nothing, but with all boldness, even now as always Christ will be exalted in my body, whether through life or through death. For to me to live is Christ and to die is gain. But if it is to live in the flesh, this is fruitful work for me, and which I will prefer I do not know. But I am hard pressed between the two options, having the desire to depart and to be with Christ, for this is very much better. But to stay on in the flesh is more necessary for your sake. And because I am convinced of this, I know that I will remain and continue with all of you for your progress and joy in the faith, so that what you can be proud of may increase in Christ Jesus because of me through my return again to you.

Only lead your lives in a manner worthy of the gospel of Christ, so that whether I come and see you or am absent I hear your circumstances, that you are standing firm in one spirit, with one soul contending side by side for the faith of the gospel.

Sometimes I think that if I'm reading the Bible and *don't* do a double take, then I'm not reading closely enough. I mean, there are some pretty wild stories and ideas packed into its pages. Sure, you know Daniel in the lion's den, the Israelites crossing the Red Sea, Jesus raising Lazarus from the dead ... but there are subtler passages of Scripture that might slip right past you if you aren't paying attention. Other times, you might read the same passage over and over again and find something new each time. That's the beauty of God's word.

Take today's reading, for example. In his letter to the Philippians, Paul writes, "For to me to live is Christ and to die is gain." A little sentence—short words, simple structure. But *whoa!* Pause right there. Paul just said that if he were to die, he would actually be winning. Death, in his view, would be success.

Now, maybe you're thinking, "Oh, well, that's fine for Paul. He was a super-Christian missionary whose letters ended up becoming a part of the Bible. His story isn't like mine. We're completely different people." I'd encourage you to think again: Remember what we read a couple days ago in 1 Corinthians? We learned that God often chooses the lowly and despised to do his work and represent him; we learned that *no one* who has been saved by Jesus can boast about positions or titles. It's 100 percent God's mercy and grace that brings us into his company. Nothing we do accomplishes what God can do through us.

IF JESUS IS OUR ULTIMATE PURSUIT, THEN JOINING HIM IN HEAVEN IS OUR ULTIMATE GOAL.

Yes, Paul is an extraordinary example of what it looks like to follow Jesus. But he's not some "super-Christian" while you and I, meanwhile, are relegated to some "lowly Christian" status. No, we're actually very similar. In the eyes of God, we are all called to pursue Jesus with every ounce of energy we've got. So when I hear Paul say "to die is gain," I've got the sneaking suspicion he isn't just talking about himself. He's saying that for us, too.

If Jesus is our ultimate pursuit, then joining him in heaven is our ultimate goal, our final destination, because as his children we are destined to be with him. Heaven is where he resides, and our true home is not in this earth, but with the one who created the heavens and earth. In the meantime, though, we've got work to do. Part of pursuing Jesus means sharing him with others and living a life that exudes traits of a Christ follower. People will start to notice Jesus through your actions when you are truly pursuing him.

GO FURTHER

What does it mean to be a citizen of heaven?

_____

_____

_____

_____

_____

If we truly are citizens of heaven, does this mean that we cannot relate to the world, or even interact with the surrounding culture?

_____

_____

_____

_____

_____

In what ways can we be citizens of heaven but still love and interact with those who aren't pursuing God—all without compromising our core beliefs and relationship with God?

_____

_____

_____

_____

_____

DAY 5.
POURING YOURSELF INTO OTHERS

2 Timothy 1:3–12

*I am thankful to God, whom I have served with a clear con-
science as my ancestors did, when I remember you constantly in my prayers night and day, longing to see you
as I remember your tears, so that I may be filled with joy,
remembering the sincere faith in you, which lived first in
your grandmother Lois and your mother Eunice, and I am
convinced that is in you also, for which reason I remind you
to rekindle the gift of God that is in you through the laying
on of my hands. For God has not given us a spirit of cow-
ardice, but of power and love and self-discipline.*

*Therefore, do not be ashamed of the testimony about
our Lord, nor me his prisoner, but suffer along with me for
the gospel, according to the power of God, who saved us and
called us with a holy calling, not according to our works but
according to his own purpose and grace that was given to
us in Christ Jesus before time began, but has now been dis-
closed by the appearing of our Savior Jesus Christ, who has
abolished death and brought to light life and immortality
through the gospel, for which I was appointed a proclaimer
and an apostle and a teacher, for which reason also I suffer these things. But I am not ashamed, because I know in*

whom I have believed, and I am convinced that he is able to guard what I have entrusted until that day.

The last few days we've read several excerpts from Paul's letters. Throughout his writing, there's such a sense of joy, wonder, and celebration of the goodness of God that it's easy to forget that Paul spent about five-and-a-half to six years in prison. I don't know about you, but I think I would have a hard time being so encouraging and uplifting if I were writing from a dark, musty prison cell. I think anybody would.

In today's passage, we not only read Paul's praises from prison, but this time we get to read the thoughts of a man facing what he likely knew to be his final months on earth. Shortly after writing this letter to Timothy, Paul became a martyr, killed for the sake of his faith in Jesus. In this trying time, Paul wrote out of steadfast love and encouragement. His words are powerful, time-less, and audacious.

In this final letter, Paul pours himself into Timothy's wondrous pursuit of God—mentoring, if you will. He reminds Timothy that he, Paul, has laid hands on Timothy, imparting Timothy with the gifts of God. The relationship between Paul and Timothy is disci-pleship at its finest. Paul then goes on to say that God gives us power, love, and self-discipline, so there's no reason to be ashamed of the fact that Paul is currently in prison. Paul isn't embarrassed or conflicted about his current state. Instead, he continues to be profound in his words, in his boldness, and in his pursuit of God.

His pursuit gives him a sense of purpose in spite of his current surroundings.

When you stop and think about it, it's a beautiful scene. As Paul's wondrous pursuit comes to a close, he exerts his final energy into supporting Timothy's wondrous pursuit. Following Jesus isn't a solo project, but instead should be done in community with fellow believers. It's crucial to have others in your life that can join you in prayer, and the pursuit of all things good. Following Jesus should be a shared experience.

FOLLOWING JESUS ISN'T A SOLO PROJECT.

Clearly, this is important to Paul, too—he opens his letter to Timothy with a reminder of his family's tradition and legacy.

Today, I encourage you to think about how you can support someone else in their wondrous pursuit of Jesus. How can you make chasing after Jesus a shared, communal activity? How can you help someone else deepen their spiritual roots?

GO FURTHER

Name two or three people who have poured into your spiritual life. How did they help you grow? Are you still in contact with them? What about their friendship made an impact on you?

_____

_____

_____

_____

_____

_____

_____

Are you currently pouring into, leading, teaching, and helping someone with his or her relationship with God?

_____

_____

_____

_____

_____

In what ways can we pour into others, in addition to pointing them to the Bible and to a church?

_____

_____

_____

_____

_____

DAY 6.
GOD IS ON YOUR SIDE

James 1:2–18

Consider it all joy, my brothers, whenever you encounter various trials, because you know that the testing of your faith produces endurance. And let endurance have its perfect effect, so that you may be mature and complete, lacking in nothing.

Now if any of you lacks wisdom, let him ask for it from God, who gives to all without reservation and not reproaching, and it will be given to him. But let him ask for it in faith, without any doubting, for the one who doubts is like the surf of the sea, driven by the wind and tossed about. For that person must not suppose that he will receive anything from the Lord; he is a double-minded man, unstable in all his ways.

Now let the brother of humble circumstances boast in his high position, but the rich person in his humiliation, because he will pass away like a flower of the grass. For the sun rises with its burning heat and dries up the grass, and its flower falls off, and the beauty of its appearance is lost. So also the rich person in his pursuits will wither away.

Blessed is the person who endures testing, because when he is approved he will receive the crown of life that he has promised to those who love him. No one who is

*being tempted should say, "I am being tempted by God,"
for God cannot be tempted by evil, and he himself tempts
no one. But each one is tempted when he is dragged away
and enticed by his own desires. Then desire, after it has con-
ceived, gives birth to sin, and sin, when it is brought to com-
pletion, gives birth to death.*

*Do not be deceived, my dear brothers. Every good gift
and every perfect gift is from above, coming down from the
Father of lights, with whom there is no variation or shadow
of change. By his will he gave birth to us through the message of truth, so that we should be a kind of first fruits of
his creatures.*

Over the last few days, we've taken a close look at the
various challenges Paul faced in his wondrous pursuit of
God. While Paul's insatiable appetite for God was truly
exceptional, all Christians should expect setbacks like
the ones he experienced. It's just part of the Christian
life. We should expect to face opposition.

When you chase after God, expect Satan to try to get
in your way. The harder you chase, the harder he'll try
to throw you off course. Satan would love nothing more
than to stop your pursuit of God—largely by keeping
you busy with petty things that don't really matter.

In today's reading, we're told to consider our trials
"all joy." They remind us that what we're doing with our
lives—our *pursuit*—matters. It's not just a hobby or a
game. This wondrous pursuit is life itself.

As you go about your pursuit, how can you discern
between the truth of God and other forces not of God?
The author of James has an answer for that: "if any of

you lacks wisdom," he says, "ask for it from God, who gives to all without reservation and not reproaching, and it will be given to [you]" (v. 5).

Just ask. God is on your side. He wants to be with you. He wants to have a relationship with you. Some of you may be wondering, "Is it really that simple?" To an extent, yes! If you want to know more, then ask more. If you want to experience more, then do more. Let your faith be active, constantly in pursuit to learn more and become stronger through God's wisdom and direction.

Sometimes, when we talk about "pursuit," our perspectives become skewed. The word "pursuit" implies a chase, right? And typically the thing you're chasing is *moving away* from you. But our pursuit of God isn't like that. God isn't moving away from us. He's actually *running toward* us. If the act of sending Jesus, God in the flesh, isn't a blatant sign that God is running toward his people, then I don't know what is.

IF YOU WANT TO KNOW MORE, THEN ASK MORE.

Today, reflect on the truth that God is on your side in this pursuit. Remember that as trials and temptations arise, he will help you discern truth, persevere, and resist Satan's schemes. Ask God to protect you in your pursuit of him. And remember that you aren't the only one in this chase; he's also chasing after you.

GO FURTHER

Share a time when you truly felt like God was on your side. How did you see his assistance in your life? Could you have made it through the situation without him?

_____

_____

_____

_____

_____

It's not always easy to trust God when we face trials and tribulations, but it's always worth it. Share a time where you found this to be true.

_____

_____

_____

_____

_____

DAY 7.
CHRIST WITH ME,
CHRIST BEFORE ME

Romans 3:21–28

But now, apart from the law, the righteousness of God has been revealed, being testified about by the law and the prophets—that is, the righteousness of God through faith in Jesus Christ to all who believe. For there is no distinction, for all have sinned and fall short of the glory of God, being justified as a gift by his grace, through the redemption which is in Christ Jesus, whom God made publicly available as the mercy seat through faith in his blood, for a demonstration of his righteousness, because of the passing over of previously committed sins, in the forbearance of God, for the demonstration of his righteousness in the present time, so that he should be just and the one who justifies the person by faith in Jesus.

Therefore, where is boasting? It has been excluded. By what kind of law? Of works? No, but by a law of faith. For we consider a person to be justified by faith apart from the works of the law.

Yesterday we reflected on the truth that God is on our side in this pursuit. He's running with us ... *to* us. We can't fully participate in the pursuit on our own. If we try to lean on our own strength, which so many of us have done time and time again, we'll eventually fail ourselves and those around us. In order to truly find our inner strength, we must realize that this strength doesn't actually come from us, but instead from God. His strength will keep us going. His strength will allow us to conquer the many trials in life. His strength will give us what we need to live a life of holiness and faithfulness. We have to learn to lean on him—to allow ourselves to be enveloped by the awesome love, power, and grace of God.

There's a beautiful Irish prayer attributed to St. Patrick that perfectly captures this idea of being totally surrounded by Christ. Allow these lines to wash over you:

> *Christ with me, Christ before me,*
> *Christ behind me,*
> *Christ in me, Christ beneath me,*
> *Christ above me,*
> *Christ on my right, Christ on my left,*
> *Christ when I lie down, Christ when I sit,*
> *Christ when I stand,*
> *Christ in the heart of everyone who thinks of me,*
> *Christ in the mouth of everyone who speaks of me,*
> *Christ in every eye that sees me,*
> *Christ in every ear that hears me.*

What would your pursuit look like if this became your prayer? When we allow Jesus to permeate every aspect of our lives, our pursuit changes.

No longer do we have to ask ourselves such futile questions as, "Am I strong enough? Am I determined enough? Am I righteous enough? Am I good enough for this pursuit?" The answer is always, "No, I'm not, but Jesus is." And that's all that matters.

ON OUR OWN, WE CAN DO NOTHING.

He accepts us in spite of our flaws and imperfections. And in today's Scripture reading, we're reminded that all people have fallen short of the glory of God, yet all are justified freely by his grace and love. We don't have to make ourselves holy and perfect. (We can't.) Our job is to chase after God and allow Jesus to soak into our lives in the way of St. Patrick's prayer. It's in that soaking process, in the continual engagement with God, that he sanctifies us.

On our own, we can do nothing. As we walk with God, however, we become sanctified. He alone has the power to complete our pursuit.

GO FURTHER

Is there such thing as a halfhearted pursuit of God?

_____

_____

_____

_____

_____

Can true transformation happen when we only seek
God part-time?

_____

_____

_____

_____

_____

Will we be able to obtain perfection in this lifetime?
If not, then why do we pursue God in the first place?
What benefit is there in chasing after something we
cannot obtain?

_____

_____

_____

_____

_____

DAY 8.
FOR YOU ARE WITH ME

Psalm 23 NIV

The LORD is my shepherd, I lack nothing.
*   He makes me lie down in green pastures,*
he leads me beside quiet waters,
*   he refreshes my soul.*
He guides me along the right paths
*   for his name's sake.*
Even though I walk
*   through the darkest valley,*
I will fear no evil,
*   for you are with me;*
your rod and your staff,
*   they comfort me.*

You prepare a table before me
*   in the presence of my enemies.*
You anoint my head with oil;
*   my cup overflows.*
Surely your goodness and love will follow me
*   all the days of my life,*
and I will dwell in the house of the LORD
*   forever.*

There were many times that King David's pursuit of God was anything but wondrous. Take, for example, the time he slept with the wife of one of his soldiers while her husband was away at battle. Or when he *then* had that soldier killed in a clumsy attempt to cover up his own sin of adultery. There's nothing "wondrous" about those actions. There's not even a trace of "pursuit" to be seen here. These are times of brokenness and frail faith.

Yet in Acts 13:22, David is called a man "in accordance with [God's] heart." How could an adulterous murderer be called a man after God's own heart? Seems puzzling to me, from the outside looking in. How could a man with so much brokenness be found faithful and attractive in God's eyes? Despite his many flaws and mistakes, David was repentant. In Psalm 25:11, David prays, "For the sake of your name, O Yahweh, forgive my sin, because it is great."

David is a paradox. His wondrous pursuit is complicated. It's messy and imperfect. It soared to the highest and fell to the lowest points possible. If we're honest with ourselves, our own lives

ASK GOD TO OPEN YOUR HEART TO THE WISDOM FOUND IN THIS PRAYER.

probably aren't too far from this truth. Like David, we have sinned against God. Also like David, we have probably brought glory to God through some—but certainly not all—of our actions.

Throughout life's ups and downs, David prayed, modeling for believers some of the strongest prayers in all of history. Without a doubt, Psalm 23 is his best-known prayer. Psalm 23 has served as an anchor in the lives of many Christians as they live out their wondrous pursuit of Jesus. It's a prayer of comfort and peace as well as one of praise and thanksgiving. Today, spend some time reading Psalm 23 slowly. Ask God to open your heart to the wisdom found in this prayer.

GO FURTHER

Share a time where you truly felt God was with you through a tough situation. How did he help? How did he direct you?

_____

_____

_____

_____

_____

Write down a time when you didn't rely on God's help. What happened in the end? Were you able to keep everything together on your own?

_____

_____

_____

_____

_____

DAY 9.
AT DEATH'S DOOR

1 Kings 17:8–16

Then the word of Yahweh came to him, saying, "Get up and go to Zarephath which belongs to Sidon and stay there. Look, I have commanded a woman there, a widow, to sustain you." So he arose and went to Zarephath and came to the gate of the city. There was a widow woman gathering wood, so he called to her, and he said, "Please bring a little water for me in a vessel so that I can drink." She went to fetch it, and he called to her and said, "Please bring me a morsel of bread in your hand." She said, "As Yahweh your God lives, surely I do not have a cake, but only a handful of flour in the jar and a little olive oil in the jug. Here I am gathering a few pieces of wood, and I will go and prepare it for me and my son, that we might eat it and die." Elijah said to her, "Don't be afraid. Go and do according to your word; only make for me a small bread cake from it first, and bring it out to me. Make it for yourself and for your son afterward. For thus says Yahweh, the God of Israel: 'The jar of flour will not be emptied and the jug of olive oil will not run out until the day Yahweh gives rain on the surface of the earth.'" So she went and did according to the word of Elijah; then both she and he ate with her household for many days. The jar of flour was not emptied and the jug of olive oil

*did not run out, according to the word of Yahweh which he
spoke by the hand of Elijah.*

Has there ever been a time in your life when you
thought your pursuit of God might lead to your *death*?
Unless you're a missionary in a restricted country, it's
probably safe to say you've never had to seriously
worry that following Jesus would be the death of you.
(Although if you've had food poisoning on a mission
trip in a third-world country, you might beg to differ!
Trust me, I've been there—after coming home from a
trip to Nicaragua, I fell extremely ill and found myself in
and out of the emergency room for almost three weeks.
It was not fun. But even then, it's nothing compared to
what others around the world face each and every day
for their faith.)

In today's Scripture, Elijah asks a widow to make
him bread from the last handful of flour and drops of
oil she has left. She wasn't just "running low" and about
to head out to the market either. This woman was pre-
paring to make a small meal for herself and her son and
then *die*. She was past the point of hope. She had nothing. And here was Elijah, telling her to make *him* some
bread. If she makes him something to eat, he says, then
God will make sure the flour and olive oil don't run out.

I don't know about you, but I would be skeptical.
Put yourself in this woman's shoes. It's hard to even
imagine, but try. Your pantry, refrigerator, freezer—
everything—is empty. Gone. You have no money.
No energy. No transportation. And even if you *did*, there
are no grocery stores, no nonprofit organizations to
offer relief, not even a farm you could steal food from.

You're starving. You've stretched all of your supplies as far as they can go, and you have one small can of food left. Then, a stranger shows up and has the audacity to say, "God says you should give me that last can. But don't worry. If you give it to me, he'll replace it and make sure it doesn't run out."

... Right.

And yet, this woman *does*. She shares her last bit of food with him, and God follows through on his promise. At death's door, the widow throws every last ounce of faith into believing Elijah speaks the truth. Her trust in God was relentless. And God provided for her.

Realize: no matter what you're facing in life, God will provide what he believes is best for you. It may not always make sense in the moment, but God will constantly contradict our own expectations in the service of his best for our lives. Whether, to you, this means finances, wisdom, or even relational help, God will hand you the tools necessary to fix what is broken, and greatly strengthen what is already good. Have faith that he will provide, and realize that faith without action is dead.

GOD WILL HAND YOU THE TOOLS NECESSARY TO FIX WHAT IS BROKEN, AND GREATLY STRENGTHEN WHAT IS ALREADY GOOD.

GO FURTHER

Share a time when you saw persecution take place.

_____

_____

Can you truly say you've personally experienced persecution in your lifetime?

_____

_____

_____

_____

_____

Are you using your personal influence—online and in person—to vocalize what's happening to other Christians all around the world—the atrocities that are taking place?

_____

_____

_____

_____

_____

DAY 10.
WORK WITH YOUR HANDS

1 Thessalonians 4:1–12

Finally therefore, brothers, we ask you and appeal to you in the Lord Jesus that, just as you have received from us how it is necessary for you to live and to please God, just as indeed you are living, that you progress even more. For you know what commands we gave to you through the Lord Jesus. For this is the will of God, your sanctification: that you abstain from sexual immorality; that each of you know how to possess his own vessel in sanctification and honor, not in lustful passion, just as also the Gentiles who do not know God; not to transgress and to exploit his brother in the matter, because the Lord is the one who avenges concerning all these things, just as also we told you beforehand and testified solemnly. For God did not call us to impurity, but in holiness. Therefore the one who rejects this is not rejecting man, but God, who also gives his Holy Spirit to you.

But concerning brotherly love, I do not have need to write to you, for you yourselves are taught by God to love one another, for indeed you are practicing it toward all the brothers in all of Macedonia. But we urge you, brothers, to progress even more, and to aspire to live a quiet life, and to attend to your own business, and to work with your hands, just as we commanded you, so that you may live decently toward those outside, and may have need of nothing.

Live a quiet life, mind your own business, and work with your hands. Sounds like something off an inspirational poster you find in a doctor's office, right? It's actually a command in the Bible. In this chapter, Paul writes to the Thessalonians, encouraging them to lead lives that are pleasing to God. Love all people, he says. But don't forget to also take care of the basic practicalities of life. Seems universally applicable, if you ask me.

Some Bible scholars believe that Paul wrote this letter to a group of people who were so certain that Jesus would be back any day now that they were abandoning their own work and communities. This behavior, in turn, put an undue burden on their neighbors. Just imagine what a mess we would have if every Christian in the United States decided tomorrow, "I don't need to work hard and save for retirement. Jesus will be back by then. And if he isn't, well someone else will take care of me." Chaos!

WORKING HARD AT YOUR JOB AND PUTTING A ROOF OVER YOUR FAMILY'S HEAD MAY NOT SEEM LIKE "WONDROUS" TASKS, BUT THEY ARE.

Should we remain in constant anticipation of the return of Christ? Absolutely! Jesus tells us in Matthew 25:13 to keep watch because we "do not know the day or the hour" he will return. But that doesn't mean we should let our homes, families, communities, and God's kingdom here on earth languish while we wait. Part of our job on this planet is to bring God's kingdom to those who don't know him, and take care of what God has graciously gifted us in this world—everything. The car you drive, the roof over your head, the food on your table, and even the clothes on your back—it's all from him. Regardless of how big or small, God has provided everything for you.

The wondrous pursuit is a spiritual one, yes, but it has many practical and physical implications. Working hard at your job and putting a roof over your family's head may not seem like "wondrous" tasks, but they are. Without taking care of life's fundamentals, how can we honestly say we're "all in" for those who make up God's kingdom?

GO FURTHER

What does it mean to live a quiet life? Should we keep silent about our relationship with God? If not, explain why.

_____

_____

_____

_____

_____

_____

The Bible says we are to live a life that is pleasing to God. Do you think your life is pleasing to God? Is there room for improvement? If so, explain how.

_____

_____

_____

_____

_____

Is there anything in the Bible that talks about needing to please people?

_____

_____

_____

_____

_____

Discuss a time when you felt yourself leaning toward pleasing people more than God.

_____

_____

_____

_____

_____

DAY 11.
"IN" THE WORLD OR "OF" THE WORLD?

1 John 2:15–17

Do not love the world or the things in the world. If anyone loves the world, the love of the Father is not in him, because everything that is in the world—the desire of the flesh and the desire of the eyes and the arrogance of material possessions—is not from the Father, but is from the world. And the world is passing away, and its desire, but the one who does the will of God remains forever.

Yesterday we explored the importance of being a part of the world. But that doesn't mean we're to love the things of the world more than we love God. In 1 John we're reminded that "the world is passing away, and its desire, but the one who does the will of God remains forever."

There's a popular phrase in churches that says, "Christians should be *in* the world, not *of* the world." Unfortunately, many Christians avoid like the plague anything that even hints of "secularism." There's a tendency in many Christian cultures to stay inside the bounds: to have only Christian friends, listen only to Christian music, see only Christian movies, etc. Obviously, having a strong Christian community is a wonderful thing. But if the only people and culture you can relate to are "Christian," then we might have a problem. We need to make sure we are both relevant to the world and seeking the righteousness of Christ at the same time. Both are doable and there is a beautiful medium that can be found in the midst of both.

GOD DIDN'T ISOLATE HIMSELF FROM THE WORLD; NEITHER SHOULD WE.

God didn't isolate himself from the world; neither should we. He inserted himself directly into its midst in a painful, beautiful, and wildly disruptive way: by becoming human. Jesus' ministry wasn't just for God's people, the Jews, either. Time and again, we see Jesus seeking out tax collectors, prostitutes, criminals, adulterers, the poor, widows, children, and even the dead (Lazarus).

Jesus waded waist deep through the world's trash. He was very much "in" the world but not "of" it. As you continue in your wondrous pursuit of God, pray that he will give you wisdom to become the person he has called you to be on this earth. Pray that he will guard you from sinful desires (like lust and pride, as mentioned in today's reading from 1 John), but also give you opportunities to influence the world around you.

GO FURTHER

Is there a healthy balance between being a follower of Jesus and still living in the world? Explain.

_____

_____

_____

_____

How can we make sure that our lives are not affected by the world's standards while still holding to biblical truth?

_____

_____

_____

_____

_____

What are the dangers of immersing yourself in the world? What could be the benefits, if there are any?

_____

_____

_____

_____

_____

DAY 12.
WHEN THE WORLD TELLS YOU YOU'RE CRAZY

John 8:12–19

Then Jesus spoke to them again, saying, "I am the light of the world! The one who follows me will never walk in darkness, but will have the light of life." So the Pharisees said to him, "You testify concerning yourself! Your testimony is not true." Jesus answered and said to them, "Even if I testify concerning myself, my testimony is true, because I know where I have come from and where I am going. But you do not know where I have come from or where I am going. You judge according to externals; I do not judge anyone. But even if I judge, my judgment is true, because I am not alone, but I and the Father who sent me. And even in your law it is written that the testimony of two men is true. I am the one who testifies concerning myself, and the Father who sent me testifies concerning me."

So they were saying to him, "Where is your father?" Jesus replied, "You know neither me nor my Father! If you had known me, you would have known my Father also."

T here will be days during your wondrous pursuit of God when the world wants you to think that you're crazy. Flat-out wrong. Irrelevant. Foolish. Ignorant. Hateful. Uncultured. Christians in many modern cultures aren't persecuted violently, but they still face persecution from plenty of people's hateful words. (Heck, there are a lot of Christians persecuting *other* Christians simply because they don't agree with them.) Social media allows a lot of this to happen.

Jesus provides a wonderful example of how to handle persecution in John 8:12–19. When the Pharisees challenge his testimony, Jesus replies, "My testimony is true, because I know where I have come from and where I am going." He tells the Pharisees that he has the testimony of the Father to support him. I mean, what more do you need?

> WHEN YOU FEEL LIKE GIVING UP ON YOUR WONDROUS PURSUIT, REMEMBER THAT GOD IS FOR YOU.

On the days when you feel like giving up on your wondrous pursuit, remember that God is for you. God is truth, and when you pursue him, you stand on the side of truth. Of course, a really important disclaimer is necessary here: this doesn't mean you're always right! And it's definitely not an excuse for pride or arrogance. Christians are every bit as capable as anyone else of creating convenient truths that suit their situation. But when the issue at hand is prayerfully considered, evaluated in light of Scripture, and found to be true, you can have peace knowing that God is on your side.

Today, I want you to think of a time someone challenged your faith. What caused them to challenge it?

How did you react? How would you handle the situation differently if it happened today?

GO FURTHER

Does your life look different from that of someone who isn't a follower of God? If so, explain how. In what ways should someone who is a Christian live differently than someone who isn't?

_____

_____

_____

_____

_____

Has anyone noticed that you are someone pursuing God without you telling them? How did they figure it out? Was it apparent, or did they have to do some searching?

_____

_____

_____

_____

_____

What are some reasons the world calls Christians crazy? If applicable, share a time where someone called you crazy for being a follower of Jesus.

_____

_____

_____

_____

_____

DAY 13.
BE STRONG AND COURAGEOUS

Joshua 1:1–9

After the death of Moses the servant of Yahweh, Yahweh said to Joshua son of Nun, the assistant of Moses, saying, "My servant Moses is dead. Get up and cross the Jordan, you and all this people, into the land that I am giving to them, to the Israelites. Every place that the soles of your feet will tread, I have given it to you, as I promised to Moses. From the wilderness and the Lebanon, up to the great river, the river Euphrates, all of the land of the Hittites, and up to the great sea in the west, will be your territory. No one will stand before you all the days of your life. Just as I was with Moses, so will I be with you; I will not fail you, and I will not forsake you. Be strong and courageous, for you will give the people this land as an inheritance that I swore to their ancestors to give them. Only be strong and very courageous to observe diligently the whole law that Moses my servant commanded you. Do not turn aside from it, to the right or left, so that you may succeed wherever you go. The scroll of this law will not depart from your mouth; you will meditate on it day and night so that you may observe diligently all that is written in it. For then you will succeed in your ways and prosper. Did I not command you? Be strong and courageous! Do not fear or be dismayed, for Yahweh your God is with you wherever you go."

Have you ever been called upon to do something difficult? Something that made you think, "How will I ever get this done?"

In today's Scripture reading, we see Joshua called to lead the Israelites after Moses' death. Moses was 120 years old when he died in the land of Moab after God brought him to the peak of Pisgah. At Pisgah, God told Moses, "This is the land that I swore to Abraham to Isaac and to Jacob, saying, 'To your offspring I will give it.' I have let you see it with your eyes, but you shall not cross into it" (Deut 34:4). Moses had faithfully served God and led his people for some time—almost to the finish line (the promised land)—so it's safe to say that Joshua had some big shoes to fill!

I imagine Joshua like the second-string quarterback who gets called in to run the final plays in the championship game. The team's star QB is down, and Joshua—unexpectedly—has to call the plays and lead his team to victory.

But there's something unique about Joshua's position: *he has God behind him.* "As I was with Moses, so I will be with you; I will not fail you, and I will not forsake you," the Lord says to Joshua. Such powerful promises. After God makes some big promises to Joshua, the new leader of his people, he follows up with some guidelines:

- Be strong and courageous.
- Diligently observe the whole law. Meditate on it day and night.

Three times in 1:6–9, the Lord says to Joshua, "Be strong and courageous." (Bible tip: When you hear God say something three times, that means it's pretty important!) Even though God anointed Joshua as his leader and promised him a land for his people, Joshua had to have been afraid. Any of us would have. This was a huge responsibility, and the potential for danger and death was high. But the Lord commanded him, "Be strong and courageous."

Our wondrous pursuit, like Joshua's, takes guts. It takes persistence. It takes bravery. And having strength and courage is the only way to do it. Yesterday, we heard that God is on our side. And just as he said to Joshua, "I will not fail you, and I will not forsake you," he says the same to you.

> OUR WONDROUS PURSUIT, LIKE JOSHUA'S, TAKES GUTS. IT TAKES PERSISTENCE. IT TAKES BRAVERY.

God's plan may not be clear or visible to you. There might be parts that don't seem to make any sense at all. And there might be times when you feel alone or abandoned. But I promise you, keep meeting God in prayer, keep active in worship, keep putting your trust in him, and keep pursuing him with reckless abandon, and you'll find a well of strength and courage. If God could give it to Joshua, he can give it to you.

GO FURTHER

Discuss a time when you were strong and courageous. What happened? Where were you? Did you overcome the obstacle at hand?

_____

_____

_____

_____

_____

There are many examples in the Bible of individuals who were strong and courageous in the name of the Lord. Share some of your favorites. What about these stories stood out to you? How can you relate?

_____

_____

_____

_____

_____

DAY 14.
ENRICH YOUR KNOWLEDGE OF GOD

2 Peter 1:3–11

His divine power has bestowed on us all things that are necessary for life and godliness, through the knowledge of the one who called us by his own glory and excellence of character, through which things he has bestowed on us his precious and very great promises, so that through these you may become sharers of the divine nature after escaping from the corruption that is in the world because of evil desire, and for this same reason, and by applying all diligence, supply with your faith excellence of character, and with excellence of character, knowledge, and with knowledge, self-control, and with self-control, patient endurance, and with patient endurance, godliness, and with godliness, brotherly love, and with brotherly love, love.

For if these things are yours and are increasing, this does not make you useless or unproductive in the knowledge of our Lord Jesus Christ. For the one for whom these things are not present is blind, being nearsighted, having forgotten the cleansing of his former sins. Therefore, brothers, be zealous even more to make your calling and election secure, because if you do these things, you will never ever stumble. For in this way entrance into the eternal kingdom of our Lord and Savior Jesus Christ will be richly supplied for you.

The wondrous pursuit starts with faith. One day, you believe. It might have been fast or gradual, sudden or a long time coming. But one day, you became a firm believer—you reached a place in your spiritual journey where you could say your actions and decisions truly all derive from a foundation in which God is what holds you together. You turned your life over to God.

So how do you add to that faith? How do you grow deeper and wider in spiritual strength? In 2 Peter we receive a list of qualities that will enrich our knowledge of Jesus:

- excellence of character
- knowledge
- self-control
- patient endurance
- godliness
- brotherly love
- love

Without these things, says Peter, we become "near-sighted and blind, forgetting that [we] have been cleansed from [our] past sins" (2 Pet 1:9 NIV). These qualities Peter lists are essential for heightening our pursuit of God. They are essential for our roots to grow deep in the soil of God's righteousness.

Today, take some time to reflect on these attributes. Maybe you don't think of yourself as very "knowledge-able" about Jesus or very good with "self-control."

But remember the opening line of today's reading: God has given us everything we need for a godly life. All of the tools, all of the building blocks, have been given to us. It's our work to uncover them through prayer and spending time in God's word.

GOD HAS GIVEN US EVERYTHING WE NEED FOR A GODLY LIFE.

Remember what God said to Joshua? "I will not fail you, and I will not forsake you. Be strong and courageous." Even more than that, he's given us everything we need to *thrive* in our pursuit of him! Make one of the qualities Peter mentioned in this reading your prayer for today. Ask God to deepen your understanding of that quality and to strengthen you in your practice of it.

GO FURTHER

Discuss ways in which you are currently deepening your relationship with God. (Books? School? Community groups?)

_____

_____

_____

_____

_____

Evaluate the ways in which you're nourishing your spiritual roots. Which are helping the most? Which are helping the least?

_____

_____

_____

_____

_____

All of the tools needed to grow deeper in our relationship with God have been given to us. How can you help others on their journeys of faith?

_____

_____

_____

_____

_____

DAY 15.
GOD AMID THE SILENCE

Mark 15:33–39

And when the sixth hour came, darkness came over the whole land until the ninth hour. And at the ninth hour Jesus cried out with a loud voice, "Eloi, Eloi, lema sabachthani?" *(which is translated,* "My God, my God, why have you forsaken me?"*) And some of the bystanders, when they heard it, said,* "Behold, he is summoning Elijah!" *And someone ran and filled a sponge with sour wine, put it on a reed, and gave it to him to drink, saying,* "Leave him alone! Let us see if Elijah is coming to take him down." *But Jesus uttered a loud cry and expired. And the curtain of the temple was torn in two from top to bottom. And when the centurion who was standing opposite him saw that he expired like this, he said,* "Truly this man was God's Son!"

Although heartbreaking and brutal, the death of Jesus is hands down the most beautiful act of love this world has ever seen. And while the Scriptures paint a beautifully epic timeline of this event, there is one part that has always made my heart curious—the time of God's silence while Jesus was on the cross.

Why was God silent? Where did he go? Why did he forsake Jesus?

Jesus called out with a loud voice, *"Eloi, Eloi, lema sabachthani?"*—meaning, "My God, my God, why have you forsaken me?" These words that Jesus cried out as he was hanging on the cross have been the source of much debate among Christians throughout the years. Some people teach that Jesus became sin itself and that's why God turned away from him, while others speculate that God was present but that the sin Jesus took upon himself blinded him from hearing God's voice.

Regardless of why … God's voice was absent.

I write this because I feel like many people today struggle with knowing God's voice and are curious as to whether God hears their cries. Regardless of why Jesus thought God was silent as he hung on the cross, I believe that even in God's silence there is power. We may not always understand what God is doing in the moment, but we must trust that God will provide for those who are in need and bring support for those who need it—in his timing, not ours.

I BELIEVE THAT EVEN IN GOD'S SILENCE THERE IS POWER.

There have been many times in my life where I felt God was silent but later realized that in this "silence" God was actually doing a mighty work within me—I just failed to realize it. What we perceive as God's silence in the midst of our pursuit of him isn't always the reality. We must trust that God knows what he's doing when it comes to taking care of the children he created.

Whether you have financial burdens, relationship problems, or even health issues, trust that God is always present, even amid what seems like silence. He's still there.

GO FURTHER

Has there been a time in your life when you felt like God was silent? For how long? What did you do? How did you cope with the silence?

_____

_____

_____

_____

Did your experience of silence strengthen or hurt your relationship with God?

_____

_____

_____

Share examples in the Bible when God was silent, or maybe not responding in the manner in which somebody wanted him to. How did the people in each situation respond? Did they stay faithful?

_____

_____

_____

_____

DAY 16.
A CORD OF THREE

Romans 1:8–16

First, I give thanks to my God through Jesus Christ for all of you, because your faith is being proclaimed in the whole world. For God, whom I serve with my spirit in the gospel of his Son, is my witness, how constantly I make mention of you, always asking in my prayers if somehow now at last I may succeed to come to you in the will of God. For I desire to see you, in order that I may impart some spiritual gift to you, in order to strengthen you, that is, to be encouraged together with you through our mutual faith, both yours and mine. Now I do not want you to be ignorant, brothers, that often I intended to come to you, and was prevented until now, in order that I might have some fruit among you also, just as also among the rest of the Gentiles. I am under obligation both to Greeks and to barbarians, both to the wise and to the foolish. Thus I am eager to proclaim the gospel also to you who are in Rome.

For I am not ashamed of the gospel, for it is the power of God for salvation to everyone who believes, to the Jew first and also to the Greek.

Have you ever had an accountability or prayer partner? Someone you could trust, who would check in on you no matter what? An accountability partner is one of the most powerful tools God has given us to overcome sin. When you allow yourself to become vulnerable with someone else, laying your soul bare, something profound can happen: God can come in and change your heart for the better. Accountability is key for anyone to pursue a thriving Christian life.

Ecclesiastes 4:12 really sticks out to me as an important verse on this topic. It says, "Though one may be overpowered, two can defend themselves. A cord of three strands is not quickly broken" (NIV). On our own, the evil one can manipulate us. With a partner, we can defend ourselves. But when there are *three*, Satan cannot easily break us—there is such power in this!

ONE BELIEVER PLUS ONE BELIEVER DOESN'T EQUAL TWO. BECAUSE JESUS IS THERE, 1 + 1 = 3.

It's quite possible that wise King Solomon, who was likely the author of Ecclesiastes, intended for us to read the "third" cord that joins two believers as God. In Matthew 18:20, Jesus says, "For where two or three are gathered in my name, I am there in the midst of them." How amazing is it that Jesus always joins us when we gather with another believer? We don't have to wait and hope he'll show up. He's already there. One believer plus one believer doesn't equal two. Because Jesus is there, 1 + 1 = 3.

In today's Scripture reading, Paul writes to believers in Rome, "I desire to see you, in order that I may impart some spiritual gift to you ... that is, to be encouraged together with you through our mutual faith." Paul is one of the most revered Christians in all of history. Yet he doesn't say to the Romans, "I want to see you so that I can encourage *you*." Paul acknowledges that the encouragement is mutual. He's walking the same path that the Romans are on. They're both looking to the same Jesus. They both *need each other* on this walk.

From Solomon to Jesus to Paul, we see that community and togetherness is important in the wondrous pursuit. It's key. We aren't told to do it alone. Rather, we're encouraged to support one another in the lifelong pursuit of Jesus.

> "Christian community is like the Christian's sanctification. It is a gift of God which we cannot claim. Only God knows the real state of our fellowship, of our sanctification. What may appear weak and trifling to us may be great and glorious to God. Just as the Christian should not be constantly feeling his spiritual pulse, so, too, the Christian community has not been given to us by God for us to be constantly taking its temperature. The more thankfully we daily receive what is given to us, the more surely and steadily will fellowship increase and grow from day to day as God pleases."
> —Dietrich Bonhoeffer, *Life Together*[2]

GO FURTHER

Do you have people in your life whom you call your friends or community? Who are they? Do you feel they're chasing after Jesus like you are? Are you walking together and supporting each other along the way? If not, pray that God would provide you with the right opportunity to walk with them in times of both victory and pain.

_____

_____

_____

_____

_____

In what ways can you find or create such a community of believers?

_____

_____

_____

_____

Can community be found outside of a church building? If so, explain how. What does community look like on a day-to-day basis?

_____

_____

_____

_____

_____

DAY 17.
AT THE CORE

Therefore, when you have prepared your minds for action by being self-controlled, put your hope completely in the grace that will be brought to you at the revelation of Jesus Christ. As obedient children, do not be conformed to the former desires you used to conform to in your ignorance, but as the one who called you is holy, you yourselves be holy in all your conduct, for it is written, "You will be holy, because I am holy." And if you call on him as Father who judges impartially according to each one's work, conduct yourselves with fear during the time of your temporary residence, because you know that you were redeemed from your futile way of life inherited from your ancestors not with perishable things like silver or gold, but with the precious blood of Christ, like that of an unblemished and spotless lamb who was foreknown before the foundation of the world, but has been revealed in these last times for you who through him are believing in God, who raised him from the dead and gave him glory, so that your faith and hope are in God.

Having purified your souls by your obedience to the truth for sincere brotherly love, love one another fervently from the heart, because you have been born again, not from

perishable seed but imperishable, through the living and enduring word of God. For
  "all flesh is like grass,
    and all its glory like the flower of the grass.
  The grass withers and the flower falls off,
    but the word of the Lord endures forever."
And this is the word that has been proclaimed to you.

I think the weight of Jesus' sacrifice sometimes gets lost in translation and time. The stakes involved in our wondrous pursuit are sometimes downplayed by contemporary Christian culture. In Sunday morning worship, with a high-energy band, dazzling lights, and dynamic video screens, are we really remembering how deeply serious and profound our God is? These things aren't innately wrong until they become the foundation on which we build our faith.

Don't get me wrong. I'm not knocking any particular style of worship. Traditional churches, contemporary churches, house churches—*all* churches can be guilty of covering up the profundity of God with their own veneer. No matter how it happens, we sometimes forget that God demands our love *and* our reverent fear.

That's where 1 Peter 1:17–19 cuts deep to the issue's core, reminding us that the great joy, freedom, and celebration found in the wondrous pursuit is also accompanied by gravity. Peter tells his readers to live in reverent fear. He reminds us, "You were redeemed from your futile way of life inherited from your ancestors not with perishable things like silver or gold, but with the precious blood of Christ."

Wow. We—we who were living an empty way of life—were traded for the absolutely most precious thing that ever passed into our stratosphere. Not silver or gold, says Peter, but the blood of Christ. We were traded out for the most valuable thing on the planet.

If you're with me here on day 17 of *Wondrous Pursuit*, then you probably know this already. I'm not throwing you for a loop. But if you're like me, the implications of this reality are something you have to remind yourself to carry. The weight of this exchange is too much for us to carry around on the top of our minds, so it's worth making a special point to return to it.

> [GOD'S] GIFT IS GREATER THAN ANY OTHER GOAL YOU COULD PURSUE.

God's gift is serious—I mean, incredibly and magnificently serious. He demands reverence and obedience. He demands our attention, and it's for a good reason. His wisdom and guidance surpass all understanding. His gift is greater than any other goal you could pursue. As you continue chasing after God, thank him today for the sacrifice of his Son. Meditate on the free gift of Christ's blood and sacrifice.

GO FURTHER

How often do you take time to thank God for the sacrifice his Son made on the cross?

_____

_____

_____

Can you truly say that you've allowed the message of the cross to resonate within your heart and soul?

_____

_____

_____

_____

_____

Do you find your thankfulness toward God to be expressed in more ways than just prayer? If so, how? In what ways can we show God thankfulness, other than through verbal affirmation and communication?

_____

_____

_____

_____

_____

THE ELEVATOR PITCH

Matthew 22:31–40

Now concerning the resurrection of the dead, have you not read what was spoken to you by God, who said, "I am the God of Abraham and the God of Isaac and the God of Jacob"? He is not the God of the dead, but of the living!" And when the crowds heard this, they were amazed at his teaching.

Now when the Pharisees heard that he had silenced the Sadducees, they assembled at the same place. And one of them, a legal expert, put a question to him to test him: "Teacher, which commandment is greatest in the law?" And he said to him, "'You shall love the Lord your God with all your heart and with all your soul and with all your mind.' This is the greatest and first commandment. And the second is like it: 'You shall love your neighbor as yourself.' On these two commandments depend all the law and the prophets."

There's something in business called "the elevator pitch." It's what you would tell somebody about yourself or your business if you only had thirty seconds to talk. Sure, you could probably talk for thirty *minutes*.

But if you only had thirty seconds, what would you say? How would you explain who you are and what you do?

If I had to explain the wondrous pursuit in just thirty seconds, the greatest commandment would definitely make it into that speech. This is where Jesus really boils it down for us. This is one of those bite-sized pieces of Scripture that you can spend a lifetime digesting.

> "LOVE THE LORD YOUR GOD WITH ALL YOUR HEART AND WITH ALL YOUR SOUL AND WITH ALL YOUR MIND."

Let me set the scene for you: in an attempt to trip him up and confuse him, a Pharisee who was extremely knowledgeable about the law asks Jesus, "Teacher, which commandment is greatest in the law?" Talk about a trick question! What arrogance. The Old Testament includes 613 laws! How could Jesus possibly say that *one* is more important than all the others? Is "do not kill" more important than "have no other gods before me"? Is "remember the Sabbath" more important than "honor your father and mother"?

Oddly enough, we have similar questions in today's day and age. We often wonder what aspects of the Christian life should receive more of our time and attention, or which sin is most grotesque in God's eyes. We like to have specific knowledge—but God just calls sin, sin, and good, good. He doesn't elevate or downplay one compared to another.

No doubt, when the Pharisees came up with their question for Jesus, they were thinking, "We've really got him in a rut now! Finally, we'll be able to get rid of this guy for good!"

Not quite. Jesus doesn't go down that easy.

Instead of getting caught up in the question, Jesus gave his audience an amazing answer. He said to them, "'Love the Lord your God with all your heart and with all your soul and with all your mind.' This is the greatest and first commandment. And the second is like it: 'You shall love your neighbor as yourself.' On these two commandments depend all the law and the prophets." I mean, who could argue with that? And if they did, their new title would easily be "heretic"!

Jesus throws them a massive curveball. But more than that, he leaves us with an incredible truth to live our lives by. If we focus on nothing else, we are to love God with all our heart and all our soul and all our mind. From this one focused action flows all other things attributed to the likeness of God. If we love God fully, then we will not kill, we will have no other gods, we will remember the Sabbath, and we will honor our fathers and mothers. Brilliant and beautiful, to say the least!

When we love God completely—spend time with him, listen to him, immerse ourselves in his word— and love our neighbor as ourselves, everything else will fall into place. That's why the greatest commandment would get a guaranteed slot in my wondrous pursuit elevator pitch—it's one of the simplest, yet most profound, pieces of the puzzle. It's the blueprint on which we should all model our lives.

GO FURTHER

How would you explain God, your relationship with him, and the Christian life to someone in less than thirty seconds? Practice your thirty-second pitches with someone or to yourself.

_____

_____

_____

_____

_____

Although thirty seconds isn't really enough time to do justice to the Christian life, do you feel comfortable sharing your faith with someone, given the opportunity?

_____

_____

_____

Think of a time you could have been open about your faith with someone but weren't. What kept you from sharing the heart transformation you find in Jesus?

_____

_____

_____

_____

Share a time you did express your relationship with God with someone. How did the conversation end? Do you feel like you were able to convey your pursuit of God in a clear and concise way? What would you do or say differently next time?

_____

_____

_____

_____

_____

DAY 19.
IT ALL BECAME GARBAGE

Philippians 3:1–11

Finally, my brothers, rejoice in the Lord. To write the same things to you is not troublesome to me, but is a safeguard for you. Beware of the dogs, beware of the evil workers, beware of the mutilation. For we are the circumcision, the ones who worship by the Spirit of God and boast in Christ Jesus and do not put confidence in the flesh, although I could have confidence even in the flesh.

If anyone else thinks to put confidence in the flesh, I can do so more: circumcised on the eighth day, from the nation of Israel, of the tribe of Benjamin, a Hebrew born from Hebrews, according to the law a Pharisee, according to zeal persecuting the church, according to the righteousness in the law being blameless. But whatever things were gain to me, these things I have considered loss because of Christ. More than that, I even consider all things to be loss because of the surpassing greatness of the knowledge of Christ Jesus my Lord, for the sake of whom I have suffered the loss of all things, and consider them dung, in order that I may gain Christ and may be found in him, not having my righteousness which is from the law, but which is through faith in Christ, the righteousness from God on the basis of faith, so that I may know him and the power of his

resurrection and the fellowship of his sufferings, being con-
formed to his death, if somehow I may attain to the resur-
rection from the dead.

By his culture's standards, Paul had a lot to be proud of. He was a circumcised Jew with Hebrew ancestry tracing back to the tribe of Benjamin. He was very well educated, brought up in the Pharisees' school. He was, by his own accounts, zealous in persecuting the followers of Jesus, who challenged centuries of Jewish tradition. And on top of all that, he admits that he was "blameless" in regards to his "righteousness in the law." Back in the day, Paul had it all—at least, from the outside looking in.

But he didn't have Jesus. After his encounter with God on the road to Damascus, Paul (who was then called "Saul") had his life changed forever. You could say his life finally started. He began his wondrous pursuit of Jesus.

In today's reading, Paul writes to the Philippians, "But whatever things were gain to me, these things I have considered loss because of Christ." Eagerly and willingly, Paul gave up everything that had given his life meaning—everything that had brought him power, status, and fame. Once he began following Jesus, all of those things became "dung," he says. (Other translations say "garbage." The Greek word Paul uses here describes the most worthless trash.)

TAKE A MINUTE; CHECK YOUR HEART AND ASK WHERE YOU SEEK YOUR IDENTITY.

Many of us are guilty of allowing our privilege, accomplishments, and social status to inflate our own sense of self-worth. But if we're totally honest with ourselves, very few of us have as much to boast about as Paul would have had during his day. Yet Paul, always setting the bar high, calls all of those things garbage. He finds his entire identity in Christ. All of his righteousness comes from God through faith, he writes.

If Paul's accomplishments pale in comparison to what Jesus did in his life, then shouldn't we say the same of ours? Take a minute; check your heart and ask where you seek your identity. Do you find your identity fully in Christ, or do you continue to hang on to your own accomplishments?

GO FURTHER

If you were really honest with yourself, where would you say that you find most of your self-worth in today's world? Do you find it in God? Or would you say something else—such as a job, a relationship, or your possessions—is where you find your identity?

_____

_____

_____

_____

_____

_____

_____

What other things do people find their worth in, apart from God?

_____

_____

_____

_____

_____

Other than God, will self-worth and identity in anything else truly last? If not, then why do we have such a yearning to chase those things? What about them attracts us?

_____

_____

_____

_____

_____

DAY 20.
PRESSING ON TOWARD THE GOAL

Philippians 3:12–21

Not that I have already received this, or have already been made perfect, but I press on if indeed I may lay hold of that for which also I was laid hold of by Christ. Brothers, I do not consider myself to have laid hold of it. But I do one thing, forgetting the things behind and straining toward the things ahead, I press on toward the goal for the prize of the upward call of God in Christ Jesus.

Therefore as many as are perfect, let us hold this opinion, and if you think anything differently, God will reveal this also to you. Only to what we have attained, to the same hold on. Become fellow imitators of me, brothers, and observe those who walk in this way, just as you have us as an example. For many live, of whom I spoke about to you many times, but now speak about even weeping, as the enemies of the cross of Christ, whose end is destruction, whose God is the stomach, and whose glory is in their shame, the ones who think on earthly things. For our commonwealth exists in heaven, from which also we eagerly await a savior, the Lord Jesus Christ, who will transform our humble body to be conformed to his glorious body, in accordance with the power that enables him even to subject all things to himself.

It's worth mentioning that Paul was just a man. Yes, a hugely important figure in Christian history and the author of several books of the Bible ... but still just a man. He wasn't perfect, and he didn't have his whole life figured out. He was just a man who relentlessly pursued the life-altering heart of Jesus.

In today's reading, a continuation of yesterday's, Paul clears something up right off the bat: "Not that I have already received this, or have already been made perfect, but I press on if indeed I may lay hold of that for which also I was laid hold of by Christ" (Phil 3:12). Paul is saying his wondrous pursuit is ongoing, never ending, something he will always be embarking on. It's a wonderful, sometimes-arduous, but always-fulfilling journey that never seems to thin out or become useless.

I don't know about you, but for me that's a relief. It's easy to see Paul as someone who has his spiritual life perfectly in order, but he admits here (and elsewhere) that he *hasn't* arrived at his goal. None of us have or will. We will never fully obtain everything we want out of our relationship with God because the vastness of God is too great for our minds to comprehend truly or fully. That's part of the beauty of our relationship with him. Remember, this is a *pursuit*—an ongoing chase. There isn't a twelve-step process guaranteed to land you the perfect relationship with Jesus. God is so much bigger. The depths of this intimate relationship go further than we can ever imagine.

So what advice does Paul give us? He says we should forget what is behind and strain toward what is ahead.

> FORGET WHAT IS BEHIND AND STRAIN TOWARD WHAT IS AHEAD.

Those past mistakes? Those roadblocks we've hit along the way? Those failures that fill our minds with regret? Those things shouldn't be our focus at all. Instead, we should press on toward the goal of Jesus—that's where our prize is found.

There are many things that can try to hold you back from embracing the wondrous pursuit of God. Guilt about your past, failures, insecurities, worries, and even fears can prevent you from living the life that God wants for you. But once you've confessed your sins and asked for God's forgiveness, you're free. Fully, totally free! This doesn't mean your past is removed from your mind, but it does mean your past no longer has control over your life. You've handed it to God, and God doesn't want you to dwell on the guilt of forgiven sins; he wants you to chase after him with total abandon. This may not always be the easiest thing to do, but with God by your side, all things are possible. You can't argue with that.

Is there something or someone holding you back from going "all in" on this wondrous pursuit? Pray over this situation with God, confess your struggles, and ask that he would give you full freedom to follow him completely. That's the life he wants you to live.

GO FURTHER

How does one stay focused on the goal that is God? In what ways can we continue to keep God as the central focus of our lives?

_____

_____

_____

What kinds of things can get us off course as we strive to make God the focus of our lives?

_____

_____

_____

_____

Pressing toward the goal means continuing to pursue God regardless of what's happening in our lives. Have you found this to be easier said than done? (Share a personal experience that illustrates your answer.)

_____

_____

_____

_____

_____

DAY 21.
DEALING WITH DOUBTERS

Jude 1:17–22

But you, dear friends, remember the words proclaimed beforehand by the apostles of our Lord Jesus Christ, for they said to you, "In the end time there will be scoffers following according to their own ungodly desires." These are the ones who cause divisions, worldly, not having the Spirit. But you, dear friends, by building yourselves up in your most holy faith, by praying in the Holy Spirit, keep yourselves in the love of God, looking forward to the mercy of our Lord Jesus Christ to eternal life. And have mercy on those who doubt.

Even if you wouldn't consider yourself a theologian or Bible scholar, you might be surprised how many phrases you'll recognize: "nothing new under the sun" (Eccl 1:9); "drop in a bucket" (Isa 40:15 NIV); "the end of the earth" (Deut 28:49).

Here's another: "Turn the other cheek." That's a command Jesus gives his followers for when they find themselves under attack. "Do not resist the evildoer," he says in Matthew 5:39. "Whoever strikes you on the right cheek, turn the other to him also." It's an interesting concept that has transcended time, causing many discussions and debates.

Perhaps one of the defining characteristics of a Christian is showing mercy to those who don't know Jesus. Christians aren't supposed to strike back when they're laughed at, beaten, or mocked. Instead, Christians are supposed to turn the other cheek and pray for those who are in need of grace.

TURN THE OTHER CHEEK AND PRAY FOR THOSE WHO ARE IN NEED OF GRACE.

In today's reading, Jude tells his readers, "Have mercy on those who doubt." It's a similar idea, and just as counterintuitive. Instead of arguing, fighting, or flat-out ignoring the scoffers, we're told to show them mercy. Jude tells his audience: *Yes*, there will be scoffers. *Yes*, people will try to divide you. But persevere, *and be merciful to the doubters.*

Not a single person has ever been won over to Christianity by a Christian who yelled and screamed at them for being a doubter. Rather, people are introduced to Jesus through Christians who exemplify Christ-like characteristics, Christians who show mercy, Christians who love, Christians who bring peace and comfort to conflict. That's what being a follower of Jesus is about. And all of these things take place through the people through whom Jesus is working. It's not by our own strength or power, but his.

As followers of Jesus, we're called to bring others into their own wondrous pursuit. "Go and make disciples of all the nations," Jesus tells us in Matthew 28:19. As we've already learned, the wondrous pursuit is not a private experience to be hidden away. We're called to share it, to live it! As we encounter people who scoff at us along the way, our reaction shouldn't be to retreat or fight back, but to show them mercy and love.

God has enabled us to be light to the world around us—and we're to take advantage of every minute we have in this life to make that a reality. In a world filled with hate and condemnation, be love. Be grace. Be the light that our dark and weary world so badly needs. That's what God is looking for. That's what it truly means to live a life that reflects the beauty of Jesus.

GO FURTHER

Have you ever experienced shame, hate, or condemnation from someone who claimed to be Christian? How did it make you feel? How did you respond to it?

_____

_____

_____

_____

_____

Do you believe someone can truly be transformed by the love of God and also live a lifestyle of hatred and cruelty? If not, explain why.

_____

_____

_____

_____

DAY 22.
PATIENCE AND THE SWING SET

James 5:7–12

Therefore be patient, brothers, until the coming of the Lord. Behold, the farmer waits for the precious fruit of the soil, being patient concerning it until it receives the early and late rains. You also be patient. Strengthen your hearts, because the coming of the Lord is near. Brothers, do not complain against one another, in order that you may not be judged. Behold, the judge stands before the doors! Brothers, take as an example of perseverance and endurance the prophets who spoke in the name of the Lord. Behold, we consider blessed those who have endured. You have heard about the patient endurance of Job, and you saw the outcome from the Lord, that the Lord is compassionate and merciful. Now above all, my brothers, do not swear either by heaven or by earth or by any other oath, but let your yes be yes and your no, no, in order that you may not fall under judgment.

I love taking our son to the park and letting him enjoy the awesomeness that is swinging. His facial expressions say it all, and his uncontrollable laughter lets us know that he's having the time of his life. His excitement is anything but hidden, and he loves every bit of it.

After a few adventures to the park, I noticed something. Each time his swing slowed, he would begin to make a face and kick his little legs as if to say, *"Push me higher! Push me higher!"*

My son isn't happy with being at a standstill—and I think many of us can relate to this feeling in our journeys with God. It's not that my son is being impatient; he just really enjoys the beauty of his father moving him forward again. It's exciting. It's rejuvenating. It's comforting. It's a riveting experience that begs to be longed for again and again.

How many times have you stepped back to take a look at your life and thought to yourself, "C'mon, God! Open up some new doors. Bring me new opportunities! I've been doing the same thing for a while now."

We've all been there. I'll be the first to admit that it's true of me.

Sometimes we act like little kids, kicking and flailing our legs to be pushed in the swing again. We enjoy being directed and moved forward in life by the hands of our Father in heaven. Why? Because it's exciting. It's rejuvenating. It's comforting. It's where we're meant to be.

GOD MOVES MOUNTAINS IN THE STILL MOMENTS.

My son isn't at the age where he can comprehend the idea of being patient, but I'm okay with that—at least for now. There's such an adorable innocence to him that you can't help but satisfy his excitement when asked—the innocence of his impatience to be pushed forward toward excitement and adventure, regardless of the risk at hand. But when we start to discuss impatience as it pertains to believers in Christ, we must learn to trust

God in our standstill moments. We need to have faith that he will open doors when the time is right, that he will push us to new heights when we're ready.

Today's reading notes how important it is for farmers to wait patiently for the valuable harvest to ripen. We, too, must wait patiently for God to move us at his speed and desire. The last thing we would want to do is forcefully move forward toward an unripened plan or season of life. We must allow God the time he needs to nurture and enrich the roots that anchor our lives.

We must learn to find fulfillment even in the quiet moments, because those actually might be the most influential and life-altering moments we experience in our lives. God moves mountains in the still moments. The standstill moments. The day-to-day moments. Why? Because God is moving in our lives even if we don't feel it or see it. Have patience, and learn to trust God even in the moments you wish to be moving on to the next season of life. He knows what he's doing.

GO FURTHER

Patience is sometimes easier said than done. Think of a time you had to be extremely patient. Was it tough? Was it easy?

_____

_____

_____

_____

_____

What can patience teach us about our relationship with God?

_____

_____

_____

_____

_____

Can you recall a time in the Bible when someone had to be extremely patient? What happened? Did it affect their relationship with God? Did they make it through the waiting game? What was the outcome?

_____

_____

_____

_____

_____

IT'S NOT ABOUT YOU

1 Timothy 1:12–17

I give thanks to the one who strengthens me, Christ Jesus our Lord, because he considered me faithful, placing me into ministry, although I was formerly a blasphemer and a persecutor and a violent man, but I was shown mercy because I acted ignorantly in unbelief, and the grace of our Lord abounded with the faith and love that are in Christ Jesus. The saying is trustworthy and worthy of all acceptance: Christ Jesus came into the world to save sinners, of whom I am the foremost. But because of this I was shown mercy, in order that in me foremost, Christ Jesus might demonstrate his total patience, for an example for those who are going to believe in him for eternal life. Now to the King of the ages, immortal, invisible, to the only God, be honor and glory forever and ever. Amen.

Once you become a Christian, something happens. Your life is no longer your own. The day I started living for Jesus, my life was no longer about my goals, my desires, my hopes. Instead, it all became about *God's* goals, God's desires, God's hopes for my life.

When you commit to follow Jesus, you commit to follow him fully. Revelation 3:16 speaks to this point: "Because you are lukewarm and neither hot nor cold, I am about to vomit you out of my mouth!" You can't be a lukewarm follower of Christ. As we talked about earlier, the wondrous pursuit is a chase. You have to be fervently, passionately, all *in*.

When you follow Jesus, your life is about Jesus, not about you. But oftentimes, we believers don't think this way. We view the things happening in our lives from a "me-centric" perspective. We think that God gave us that promotion because we worked hard or that God didn't cure a loved one's illness because we didn't pray enough. The truth is, God is not a transactional genie. He doesn't give to the deserving and take from the undeserving. (If he did, most of us would be in a lot of trouble!) Rather, God is almighty and sovereign with a will independent of our actions. That's not to say our prayers or choices don't matter, because they do. But they are not the ultimate controlling force in our lives. The same God that allowed Job to suffer gave Lazarus a second life on earth.

> WHEN YOU FOLLOW JESUS, YOUR LIFE IS ABOUT JESUS, NOT ABOUT YOU.

One of my favorite parts of today's reading is verse 16. Paul *gets* it. He essentially says to Timothy, "Listen, I'm the worst sinner there is, and Jesus showed me mercy so that he could use it as an example of his immense patience."

The mercy God showed Paul wasn't to glorify Paul. Instead, Paul claims that the mercy shown to him was for Jesus' own glory. Paul didn't do anything to deserve the mercy; it was something God decided to do for himself! I love that Paul shares this perspective with us.

As you continue on your wondrous pursuit, remember that whatever happens—good or bad—it isn't always about you. Sometimes God, in his infinite wisdom beyond our understanding, gives and takes from his people in order to bring glory to himself.

GO FURTHER

What does it mean to say your life is no longer your own? How does this set you up for success in your wondrous pursuit of God?

_____

_____

_____

_____

_____

Is completely handing your life over to God something you find easy? If not, why? Do you feel there will always be tension when it comes to this part of our spiritual lives?

_____

_____

_____

_____

_____

Does living a life fully devoted to God mean that we cannot accept any type of awards, promotions, or praise for the hard work we put into things? Is there something wrong with working hard and being recognized for it?

_____

_____

_____

_____

_____

If our lives are no longer our own, does this mean that our opinions, ideas, and aspirations are no longer important to God? Explain why or why not.

_____

_____

_____

_____

_____

DAY 24.
MORE THAN A BOOK

Hebrews 5:11–14

Concerning this we have much to say and it is difficult to explain, since you have become sluggish in hearing. For indeed, although you ought to be teachers by this time, you have need of someone to teach you again the beginning elements of the oracles of God, and you have need of milk, not solid food. For everyone who partakes of milk is unacquainted with the message of righteousness, because he is an infant. But solid food is for the mature, who because of practice have trained their faculties for the distinguishing of both good and evil.

When you're a second grader, Dr. Seuss is pretty incredible. The sentences are short, the words are fun, the stories are hilarious and exciting. But then you learn to read more complex sentences. You discover bigger words and richer plots. Dr. Seuss is still *good*, but it's no longer the pinnacle of your literary experience. You yearn for more. You get older and you discover deeper characters and stories. You grow. It's a totally normal part of life. The more we discover and experience in the world, the richer and more complex our desires become.

Then there's the Bible. For some reason, a lot of Christians don't actively grow in their knowledge of this amazing piece of literary art. I know it took me a while to get started. Only about eight years ago did I start reading the Bible out of pure desire and intrigue; before that, my Bible spent most of its time collecting dust on a shelf in my room. Every once in a while, I'd dust it off only to be used as an accessory while attending the yearly Christmas Eve or Easter Sunday service.

WITHOUT A SOLID FOUNDATION, WE CAN'T BUILD A SOLID RELATIONSHIP.

For much of my life, the Bible was nothing more to me than a paper-and-ink book. It wasn't until I dropped my pride that I realized this was no mere book; it was a lifeline, a safety net, a second chance, and an answer to the many questions I had about my life. I was hooked. My love for the Bible did not come easily, but the more time I spent in God's word, the more I realized how much I truly need its presence in my life.

In today's reading, the author of Hebrews chastises his audience for not even *trying* to seriously learn God's word. He tells them that they need to go back to the beginning. "You need milk, not solid food!" he says. Once they get the basics right, they'll be ready to move on to the more complex stuff.

The same goes for us. It's our job to spend time in the Bible, learning God's word. We must take time to learn the basics before diving headfirst into the Bible's many complexities. Only then can we expand our knowledge—without a solid foundation, we can't build a solid relationship. Though we have less than a week left in *Wondrous Pursuit*, it's my prayer that you'll continue exploring the Bible and learning about God on your own.

GO FURTHER

What is the Bible to you? How do you describe it to others?

_____

_____

_____

_____

_____

_____

How does the Bible differ from any other book or piece of literature? Why is it so unique?

_____

_____

_____

_____

_____

_____

_____

How regularly do you read your Bible? Are you reading it out of duty or desire?

_____

_____

_____

_____

_____

DAY 25.
TWO MASTERS

Romans 6:1–23

What therefore shall we say? Shall we continue in sin, in order that grace may increase? May it never be! How can we who died to sin still live in it? Or do you not know that as many as were baptized into Christ Jesus were baptized into his death? Therefore we have been buried with him through baptism into death, in order that just as Christ was raised from the dead through the glory of the Father, so also we may live a new way of life. For if we have become identified with him in the likeness of his death, certainly also we will be identified with him in the likeness of his resurrection, knowing this, that our old man was crucified together with him, in order that the body of sin may be done away with, that we may no longer be enslaved to sin. For the one who has died has been freed from sin.

Now if we died with Christ, we believe that we will also live with him, knowing that Christ, because he has been raised from the dead, is going to die no more, death no longer being master over him. For that death he died, he died to sin once and never again, but that life he lives, he lives to God. So also you, consider yourselves to be dead to sin, but alive to God in Christ Jesus.

Therefore do not let sin reign in your mortal body, so that you obey its desires, and do not present your members to sin as instruments of unrighteousness, but present yourselves to God as those who are alive from the dead, and your members to God as instruments of righteousness. For sin will not be master over you, because you are not under law, but under grace.

What then? Shall we sin because we are not under law but under grace? May it never be! Do you not know that to whomever you present yourselves as slaves for obedience, you are slaves to whomever you obey, whether sin, leading to death, or obedience, leading to righteousness? But thanks be to God that you were slaves of sin, but you have obeyed from the heart the pattern of teaching to which you were entrusted, and having been set free from sin, you became enslaved to righteousness. (I am speaking in human terms because of the weakness of your flesh.) For just as you presented your members as slaves to immorality and lawlessness, leading to lawlessness, so now present your members as slaves to righteousness, leading to sanctification. For when you were slaves of sin, you were free with respect to righteousness.

Therefore what sort of fruit did you have then, about which you are now ashamed? For the end of those things is death. But now, having been set free from sin and having been enslaved to God, you have your fruit leading to sanctification, and its end is eternal life. For the compensation due sin is death, but the gift of God is eternal life in Christ Jesus our Lord.

Grace. It's one of the most talked about aspects of Christianity—and for good reason. God's grace means that we get something we don't deserve: eternal life and freedom through the death of his Son, Jesus Christ. Does grace mean we get a free pass to do whatever we want in life? Not at all. Paul addresses this in verse 15 of today's reading and the verses that follow. Through our faith in Jesus, we have died to sin and come alive in him.

When we were sinners who did not know the Lord, Paul says, we were "free with respect to righteousness" (v. 20). Basically, our sin and lack of faith ensured our death and despair, so what did righteousness matter? But once we proclaimed our faith and received God's grace, our master changed. Our life took shape and was given purpose. Sin is no longer the master; God is. Now, in following God, we sow holiness and eternal life through our righteousness.

SIN IS NO LONGER THE MASTER; GOD IS.

This means our day-to-day lives should exude the freedom that comes from being followers of Jesus. We are to show love to those the world calls unlovable, to pray for those who are hurting, and to generously give to those who are in need.

Once dead, we were not able to fully live life the way God created us to. But since his Son was sent to die on a cross and carry the burden of our sins, we now have true freedom to live into an identity and a powerful destiny that is unshakable. God's grace has set us free, so we must take full advantage of the time we have here on earth to give the gift of the gospel to the world around us. Let your life be an active illustration of the grace and freedom that is Jesus.

GO FURTHER

In what ways could we find ourselves slaves to our sinful nature if we're not careful? Do we find examples of this in the Bible? If so, what are they?

_____

_____

_____

_____

Regardless of how much we pursue the likeness of God in this life, will we ever find ourselves fully cleansed of sin? If not, explain why.

_____

_____

_____

_____

_____

If we are incapable of fleeing from all of our sinful nature, what's the point of chasing after God in the first place?

_____

_____

_____

_____

_____

DAY 26.
THE FRUIT OF THE SPIRIT

Galatians 5:16-26

But I say, live by the Spirit, and you will never carry out the desire of the flesh. For the flesh desires against the Spirit, and the Spirit against the flesh, for these are in opposition to one another, so that whatever you want, you may not do these things. But if you are led by the Spirit, you are not under the law.

Now the deeds of the flesh are evident, which are sexual immorality, impurity, licentiousness, idolatry, sorcery, enmity, strife, jealousy, outbursts of anger, selfish ambition, dissension, factions, envy, drunkenness, carousing, and things like these, things which I am telling you in advance, just as I said before, that the ones who practice such things will not inherit the kingdom of God. But the fruit of the Spirit is love, joy, peace, patience, kindness, goodness, faithfulness, gentleness, self control. Against such things there is no law. Now those who belong to Christ have crucified the flesh together with its feelings and its desires.

If we live by the Spirit, we must also follow the Spirit. We must not become conceited, provoking one another, envying one another.

What does a real Christian look like? What qualities should a Christian display here on earth? What does it really mean to follow the direction of God's word?

The Bible doesn't leave the answer a mystery. We get a perfect description in Galatians 5:22–23. When we're actively pursuing God, the Spirit's fruits in our lives are "love, joy, peace, patience, kindness, goodness, faithfulness, gentleness, [and] self-control."

Jesus' life and ministry perfectly encapsulate all the fruits of the Spirit noted in Galatians 5. If you ever want an example of what these fruits look like, just open up any of the four Gospels and watch how Jesus handles life's many obstacles and challenges. He shows love to everyone he meets, including those who are against him. He brings joy into a world that desperately needs it. He brings peace into frightening situations like the stormy waters (Ps 107:29), and he even displays patience when his disciples continuously fail to listen to him (e.g., Mark 14:37). Jesus, in his kindness and goodness, gives freely of his time to those who ask for it, and he shows constant faithfulness when he prays all night in the garden of Gethsemane. He is gentle, welcoming the little children to him, and shows self-control throughout his forty days of temptation.

"LOVE, JOY, PEACE, PATIENCE, KINDNESS, GOODNESS, FAITHFULNESS, GENTLENESS, SELF CONTROL"

Discovering and producing the fruit of the Spirit is integral to every Christian's wondrous pursuit. Today, I encourage you to focus on one of these qualities. It can be the one that comes easiest to you, or the one you find most challenging.

Pray for opportunities to develop that quality. Ask God to keep this fruit in the front of your mind as you go about your day, and pray for opportunities to exercise this fruit daily.

The fruit of the Spirit is growing within you. As your roots grow deeper in God, your branches will grow stronger, and the fruit becomes more delicious! But growth requires good soil, nutrients, and watering. This is where faith comes into play. Meet God in prayer, worship, and through studying his word, and you just might be surprised at the results he can bring about in your pursuit of him.

GO FURTHER

Which fruits of the Spirit are you most comfortable with? Which ones do you need to work on?

_____

_____

_____

_____

_____

_____

_____

There are many people in this world who claim to pursue God yet lack many of the fruits of the Spirit. Why do you think this is?

_____

_____

_____

_____

_____

_____

_____

THE GOSPEL IN A FEW WORDS

Isaiah 40:1–11

"Comfort; comfort my people," says your God.

"Speak to the heart of Jerusalem, and call to her,

that her compulsory labor is fulfilled, that her sin is paid for,

> *that she has received from the hand of Yahweh double for all her sins."*

A voice is calling in the wilderness, "Clear the way of Yahweh!

> *Make a highway smooth in the desert for our God!*
Every valley shall be lifted up,
> *and every mountain and hill shall become low,*
And the rough ground shall be like a plain,
> *and the rugged ground like a valley-plain.*
And the glory of Yahweh shall be revealed,
> *and all humankind together shall see it,*

for the mouth of Yahweh has spoken."

A voice is saying, "Call!"
> *And he said, "What shall I call?"*

All humankind are grass,
and all his loyalty is like the flowers of the field.
Grass withers; the flower withers
when the breath of Yahweh blows on it.
Surely the people are grass.
Grass withers; the flower withers,
but the word of our God will stand forever.

Get yourself up to a high mountain, Zion, bringer of good
news!
Lift up your voice with strength, Jerusalem, bringer of
good news!
Lift it up; you must not fear!
Say to the cities of Judah, "Here is your God!"
Look! The Lord Yahweh comes with strength,
and his arm rules for him.
Look! His reward is with him,
and his recompense in his presence.
He will feed his flock like a shepherd;
he will gather the lambs in his arm,
and he will carry them in his bosom;
he will lead those who nurse.

The fact that God's word "will stand forever," outlasting everything else, is an incredible comfort to me. No matter what happens in our lives or in the world, we can rely on the truth of God and his promises to carry us. In fact, his word is the only thing we can rely on. His word can bring us to places we would have never imagined reaching. His promises are both telling and worthwhile.

The prophet Isaiah reminds us of God's gentleness and his love for us. He tells us that God carries his lambs close to his heart. He gently leads them. He takes care of them. We all hit rocky parts on the road of our wondrous pursuit. There will be times when your faith is rattled, when you feel alone, when you feel hopeless. There may be times when the people you've trusted for spiritual guidance and leadership completely fail you. During these times, you might feel like throwing in the towel.

Don't. Press forward.

People will disappoint you. Churches will disappoint you. Small groups will disappoint you. Books will disappoint you. "But the word of our God will stand forever." When you're feeling lost on your journey, when the going gets tough, turn to God's word.

The Bible is the richest, most profound text that has ever existed or ever will exist. It covers a vast number of topics, including everything from grace and love to politics, marriage, joy, peace, raising children, and more.

KEEP DIGGING INTO GOD'S WORD. IT NEVER DISAPPOINTS; IT NEVER FAILS.

As I've said before, we sometimes take it for granted that the creator of the entire universe put truth into words and then placed the pages into our hands. That's a truly special thing.

As we near the end of *Wondrous Pursuit*, I again encourage you to keep digging into God's word. It never disappoints; it never fails. It's the one thing we can count on in this world when everything else falls apart.

GO FURTHER

Think of a Bible passage that has impacted you. What about it spoke to you? How has it continued to speak to you since that first time? How has it changed your perspective on life? How has it deepened your spiritual roots?

_____

_____

_____

_____

_____

_____

Share a time where an individual has disappointed you. What happened? How did it directly affect you? Did you find encouragement in God's word? If so, which passage(s)?

_____

_____

_____

_____

_____

_____

DAY 28.
THE MUSTARD SEED

Mark 4:30–34

And he said, "With what can we compare the kingdom of God, or by what parable can we present it? It is like a mustard seed that when sown on the ground, although it is the smallest of all the seeds that are on the ground, but when it is sown it grows up and becomes the largest of all the garden herbs, and sends out large branches so that the birds of the sky are able to nest in its shade." And with many parables such as these he was speaking the word to them, as they were able to hear it. And he did not speak to them without a parable, but in private he explained everything to his own disciples.

Over the last few weeks, we've reflected on the idea that the wondrous pursuit is not a solo venture. It's personal, but it's not private. It's meant to be shared. God wants us to chase after him alongside others that are part of the body of Christ. In today's passage Jesus talks about his kingdom (the church), using the mustard seed as a parable. (Fun fact: This parable shows up in three of the four Gospels.)

Jesus says that his church is like a mustard seed— a very tiny seed that his audience would have been familiar with. On its own, a mustard seed is just a tiny sphere. You would barely be able to pinch one between two fingers. It's just a tiny speck in the vast world.

But when the mustard seed is planted, its significance does a 180-degree turn. Although the seed is tiny, from it grows a plant that is a force to be reckoned with. The black mustard plant (the plant most scholars believe Jesus would have been referring to in this parable) has a voracious appetite. It shoots out in all directions, creating thick hedges and deep roots. It's a home for many animals, and even has the unique feature of releasing chemicals that prevent some other plants from growing near it. You don't want to get in its way.

> **THE WONDROUS PURSUIT IS NOT A SOLO VENTURE. IT'S PERSONAL, BUT IT'S NOT PRIVATE.**

Jesus also tells his audience that the mustard plant is big enough for birds to perch in its shade. His point is powerful. With the right environment, dedication, and cultivation, the small kingdom that was begun by Jesus and would soon be carried out into the world by his disciples can become a mighty force that brings peace, life, and comfort to the world. This will take place when believers can come together on a massive scale, loving each other and serving the rest of the world as one body dedicated to bringing glory to Jesus.

Maybe you feel like your own pursuit is currently the size of a mustard seed. Maybe you feel like you're not exactly in the place you'd like to be as it pertains to your faith. That's okay. That's where the kingdom of God began, too.

When we plant ourselves in God's word, commune with him in prayer, and nurture relationships with others who are focused on him, that small seed can flourish into something amazing. Today, ask God how you can grow your relationship with him. What changes in your life could enrich your pursuit of him?

GO FURTHER

What does "having faith" mean to you? Think of a time when you stepped out in faith. What happened? What did you learn from the experience?

_____

_____

_____

_____

_____

James 2:17 says that faith without works is dead. What does that mean? Share an example of this truth.

_____

_____

_____

_____

_____

Is faith in God enough? If not, what also must happen to build a full relationship with him?

_____

_____

_____

_____

_____

DAY 29.
PERFECT TIMING

James 5:13–18

Is anyone among you suffering misfortune? He should pray. Is anyone cheerful? He should sing praise. Is anyone among you sick? He should summon the elders of the church and they should pray over him, anointing him with olive oil in the name of the Lord. And the prayer of faith will save the one who is sick, and the Lord will raise him up, and if he has committed sins he will be forgiven. Therefore confess your sins to one another, and pray for one another, so that you may be healed. The effective prayer of a righteous person accomplishes much. Elijah was a human being with the same nature as us, and he prayed fervently for it not to rain, and it did not rain on the land for three years and six months. And he prayed again, and the sky gave rain and the earth produced its fruit.

First Thessalonians 5:17 tells us to "pray constantly." Ephesians 6:18 says to pray "at all times." So, we shouldn't be surprised to read in today's Scripture that prayer is a necessary and good thing for many of life's circumstances.

In trouble? Pray.
Happy? Pray.
Sick? Pray.

As if to add a punctuation mark of proof, James ends with an anecdote about Elijah: Elijah prayed it wouldn't rain, and it didn't. Then he prayed that it would, and it did.

WE HAVE TO BE WILLING TO LET GO OF OUR PLANS AND INSTEAD GRAB HOLD OF THE WILL OF GOD.

Sounds easy, right? You've probably spent more than a few hours of your life praying—but I'm going to go out on a limb here and guess that those prayers didn't cause dramatic shifts in weather patterns. And despite what verse 15 says about prayers offered in faith making the sick person well, I'm going to guess that not every illness you've prayed for has resulted in a dramatic, complete recovery.

So, what gives?

Well, God works in *his* ways, not ours. And although that may be hard to swallow sometimes, it's part of the surrender required in the Christian life. If God answered all of our prayers in the way we saw fit, the world would be one scary place.

Just like any loving parent, God seeks what is best for his children and will constantly challenge our expectations for our own benefit. He knows what's best, and his ways will always be grander than our own. We have to be willing to let go of our plans and instead grab hold of the will of God. I know this concept is easier said than done, but it will always be worth it in the long run.

God's plans are perfect because God himself is perfect. He is the almighty assurance of life, guiding us toward the greatest good: his will. Although God is faithful in answering prayer, we cannot expect him to answer every prayer exactly as we want him to. Faith requires trusting him even when things don't make sense; it includes trusting him when *we* think a prayer was met with the wrong answer, the wrong timing, or was ignored. (Good news, though: God never *ignores* our prayers. "Yahweh your God is the one going with you; he will not leave you alone and he will not forsake you," says Deuteronomy 31:6.)

So, should we even bother praying? Absolutely. Jesus tells us to pray and gives us a model in Matthew 6:9–13. Today's Scripture offers more insights into how to pray well. My encouragement for you is to forget the notion that all prayers will be answered the way you want them to be. Instead, rest in the peace of knowing that God hears your prayers and will provide the answers in the perfect timing that only he can bring about.

GO FURTHER

Evaluate your prayer life (use a scale from one to ten, if you like). Share your answer with others. How can you improve your prayer life?

_____

_____

_____

_____

_____

_____

Discuss examples in the Bible where a prayer resulted in something extraordinary. Do we still see instances of this today? If so, explain.

_____

_____

_____

_____

_____

Is prayer a necessity in the Christian life? If so, why? What about it is intrinsically important to our spiritual growth as followers of Jesus?

_____

_____

_____

_____

_____

DAY 30.
MAY HIS FACE SHINE ON YOU

Ephesians 2:1–10

And you, although you were dead in your trespasses and sins, in which you formerly walked according to the course of this world, according to the ruler of the authority of the air, the spirit now working in the sons of disobedience, among whom also we all formerly lived in the desires of our flesh, doing the will of the flesh and of the mind, and we were children of wrath by nature, as also the rest of them were.

But God, being rich in mercy, because of his great love with which he loved us, and we being dead in trespasses, he made us alive together with Christ (by grace you are saved), and raised us together and seated us together in the heavenly places in Christ Jesus, in order that he might show in the coming ages the surpassing riches of his grace in kindness upon us in Christ Jesus. For by grace you are saved through faith, and this is not from yourselves, it is the gift of God; it is not from works, so that no one can boast. For we are his creation, created in Christ Jesus for good works, which God prepared beforehand, so that we may walk in them.

The benediction is an old tradition that goes back to earliest days of the church. At the end of the worship service, the priest or pastor says a short prayer, typically one directly from Scripture or out of church history, that asks for guidance or blessings for the people before they leave the church and go out into the world. The Bible, especially the New Testament letters, is full of benedictions.

Today's Scripture passage isn't technically a benediction, but it works as a beautiful, joyful, and uniting capstone to our shared experience in this wondrous pursuit. Paul reminds us, once again, that God took us from death to life, from the grave to being seated in heaven with Jesus. And not only do we get to experience a dramatic transformation, but it's through no action of our own. We were saved through grace and faith, "not from works, so that no one can boast."

How many times did the early Christians have to be reminded that their position came through *grace*—not their own righteousness? This theme pops up throughout Paul's letters. It's an issue that plenty of Christians still struggle with today. Even though we *know* we were saved by God's grace alone, we're often guilty of being self-righteous in how we treat other Christians—and those who don't know Jesus.

As this chapter of your wondrous pursuit comes to a close and you embark on the next, carry with you these two things that Paul writes at the end of today's Scripture: One, remember that your life in Christ comes from God's grace, not from anything you did to deserve it. As Christians, we are overflowing with the best gift in the world: Jesus. The fact that we didn't deserve this gift should always keep us humble.

Two, remember that you are "created in Christ Jesus for good works." The gift of Jesus wasn't given to us that we might huddle up in our homes and churches and keep him all for ourselves. The wondrous pursuit is meant to be shared. "Therefore, go and make disciples of all the nations," says Jesus (Matt 28:19).

THIS IS JUST THE BEGINNING.

Your wondrous pursuit isn't over after 30, 300, or 3,000 days. This is just the beginning. My prayer for you is that you will continue to chase madly after God. He hears his people and responds.

And now, for a benediction:

> Yahweh will bless you
>   and keep you;
> Yahweh will make shine his face on you
>   and be gracious to you;
> Yahweh will lift up his face upon you,
>   and he will give you peace. (Num 6:24–26)

GO FURTHER

Share what you have you learned about your relationship with God over the last 30 days. What has changed? What has God revealed to you?

_____

_____

_____

_____

_____

Which days in this 30-day journey have spoken to you the most? Why?

_____

_____

_____

_____

_____

How will your relationship with God be different moving forward? What do you see changing in your life? What do you see remaining the same?

_____

_____

_____

_____

_____

CONNECT WITH JARRID

Website: http://JarridWilson.com

Facebook: http://Facebook.com/JarridWilson

Twitter: @JarridWilson

Instagram: @JarridWilson

Snapchat: JarridWilson

NOTES

1. "Pursue." Merriam-Webster.com. Merriam-Webster, n.d. Web. 28 Sept. 2016.
2. Dietrich Bonhoeffer, *Life Together: The Classic Exploration of Christian Community*, trans. John W. Doberstein (New York: HarperOne, 1954), 30.